To Laurel, Aislyn, and Kiri Anne,
the three women of my life,
tall and small.

Matthias Breiter

The Bears
of Katmai
Alaska's Famous Brown Bears

Contents

"What is man without the beasts? If all the beasts were gone, man would die from a great loneliness of spirit. For whatever happens to the beasts, soon happens to man. All things are connected."

—Sealth, Chief of the Duwamish, Suquamish, and allied Indian tribes in a letter to President Franklin Pierce in 1854

Alpenglow drapes the flanks of Mount Katolinat in soft hues of red and pink

Far in the distance, on the southern horizon, Mt. Mageik stands in solitary splendor. Evidence of the fire still burning in Mageik's heart, plumes of smoke disperse in the wind swirling around its glacier-shrouded slopes. In this part of the world, **even the mountains are alive.**

Faces and voices of the wilderness: in the top of a tree beside the river, the white head of a bald eagle shines like freshly fallen snow. Foxes play tag along the shore, and on some evenings the silence is broken by the call of a wolf.

Deep imprints of strong paws join to form wide furrows. Countless bear paths, worn deeply into the thick moss carpet, traverse the woods.

**About 650 yards upstream
from the river's mouth,**
beyond an oxbow that redirects
the water's might,

the current has dug deep into a little hill, carving a cutbank out of the small rise. On top of it, a few yards above the water, I have taken up my photographic watch.

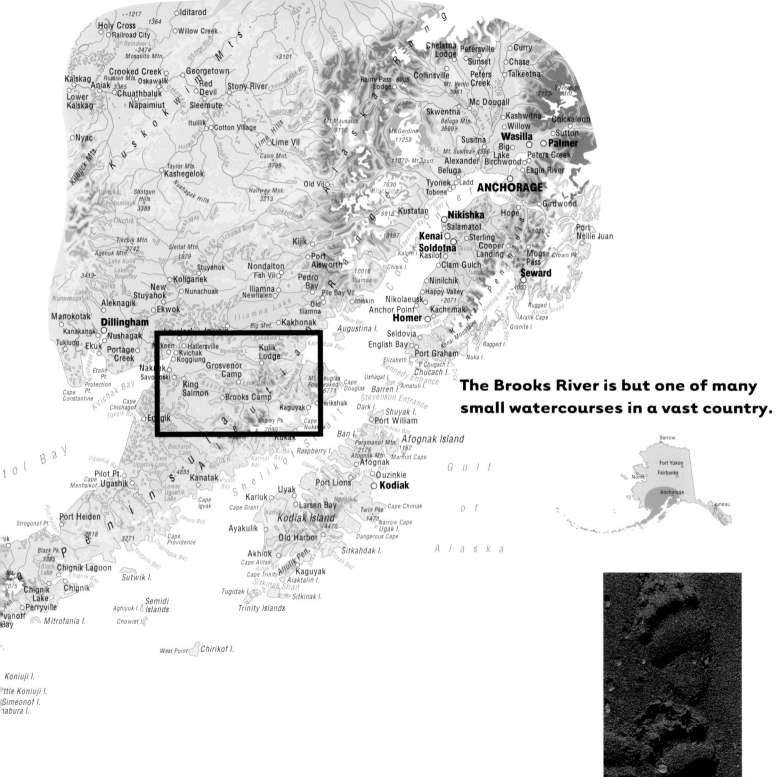

The Brooks River is but one of many small watercourses in a vast country.

19

Suddenly, a bear

Gently flowing waters separate the spit from a small island, covered with tall grass, in the middle of the river.

appears on it.

The low sun stands right behind its back, casting an aurora of light around the animal.

For a few moments, the play of light and shadow captures all my attention.

The world around exists only on the very periphery of my awareness.
Then the sound of steps in the sand penetrates my concentration, and my focus widens.

Naknek Lake lies like a turquoise mirror under a crystal blue sky. Across the lake, the broken crest of Mt. Katolinat towers above the wooded shores. Its precipitous flanks are draped in the torn, white blanket the first snow cast across the mountain a few days earlier. Far in the distance, on the southern horizon, Mt. Mageik stands in solitary splendor. The volcano abides in repose with evidence of the fire still burning in Mageik's heart. Plumes of smoke disperse in the wind swirling around its glacier-shrouded slopes. In this part of the world, even the mountains are alive.

The wind shifted last night, blowing out of the Northwest now. The cold air has pushed the heavy cloud cover of the last few days across the mountain range. The clear weather comes at the cost of moderate temperatures. Sharp frost holds the country in an icy embrace. It is late fall. On the Alaska Peninsula, the sun is no longer able to warm the land on its

low traverse across the sky. In protected bays, a fragile skin of ice grows from the shoreline out into the lake. Bundled-up, camera on my knees, I sit alone on a sandy spit at the mouth of the Brooks River. The birch trees along the bank have already dropped their leaves. Winter is close. Tomorrow I will return to King Salmon by boat. It is time. Because of ice, every trip across the huge lake, which is more than thirty miles long, will soon become a dangerous endeavor. Floatplane operators have long since ceased to offer service and have pulled their aircraft out of the water. The thermometer dropped to 5 °F last night. I savor the hours of solitude on this final afternoon.

Two weeks earlier, Greg, a friend of mine, and I had come up the treacherous waters of the lake in a little skiff. Some days we went our separate photographic ways. Today he decided to follow the Brooks River upstream, while I spent the day

A sow with two cubs sits a few yards away at the water's edge.

along its lower reaches.

Efforts to locate the Brooks River on a map are usually made in vain. It is but one of many small water courses in a vast country. At the mouth, the river is less than fifty yards wide. Its run is just one mile long, connecting Brooks Lake with Naknek Lake. Yet, every year I am inexorably drawn to this place. The clear, mineral-and-oxygen-rich streams of

Unlike myself,
the large female,
weighing about **600 pounds**,
appears to feel no discomfort whatsoever in
our mutual proximity.

the Alaska Peninsula are important spawning grounds for sockeye salmon. Each summer, in early July, they show up in huge schools in the estuary of the Naknek River. A few days later, the first salmonid vanguard arrives in the Brooks River. They come in waves of countless thousands of fish fighting the strong current in unison. Rapids slow their advance. As the first surge attempts to clear the white-water barrier, the next moves in, and soon salmon are stacked up several feet deep in the river. Lined up row upon row, their bodies appear to have replaced all water; it seems possible to cross over to the other side dry footed by walking on their backs.

The promise of a readily available meal exerts a powerful attraction on many animals. Bald Eagles sit in the tops of trees lining the river. Even wolves have been observed catching salmon here. However, most often they have to surrender their fishing spot to the monarch of the Alaskan wilderness: the brown bear. During the salmon run, more than forty bears congregate along the Brooks River to access this rich nutrition. With salmon in overabundance at paw's reach, fish becomes a fast-food item. Countless bear paths, worn deep into the thick moss carpet, traverse the woods. One of the largest brown bear concentrations in the world is found in this region. In Katmai National Park, in which the Brooks River is located, it is estimated that there are three thousand brown bears. To put this figure into perspective, the bear population density on the Alaska Peninsula is as much as 250 times higher than in areas in which bears have no access to salmon and where the climate is colder, as in Alaska's Far North. In July, up to fifteen animals can be observed along the river at one time. Due to the protein-rich diet, these bears reach enormous size; a large male may weigh as much as thirteen hundred pounds. These giants of the animal kingdom are the reason for my yearly visits to the Brooks River.

Even now, in the last days of fall, bears are still about. Apart from a few late arrivals swimming in total disregard for the masses, the migration of the sockeye salmon has come to an end for the year. However, the fish die after spawning. Half dead and already lifeless salmon are swept downstream and washed ashore where the current slackens. For a second time, Mother Nature provides a rich buffet for the bruins. And as the epitome of opportunists, they do not scorn such easy quarry.

For me, these weeks preceding the onset of winter are the restful conclusion to a hectic summer, a time to recuperate from the hurly-burly of the year past, and a time to collect myself and recharge my inner batteries in preparation for the long winter ahead. Wildlife photography is all too often a race in pursuit of dramatic images. One easily becomes a distant, detached observer. Here, I still have the opportunity to develop a personal relationship with the animals, getting to know them as individuals.

Gently flowing waters separate the spit from a

small island in the middle of the river, covered in tall grass. At this very moment, a subadult male appears on it. The low sun stands right behind its back, casting an aurora of light around the moving animal. I will miss this place.

For a few moments the play of light and shadow captures all my attention. The world around exists only on the very periphery of my awareness. Then the sound of steps in the sand penetrates my concentration and my focus widens. Expecting to find Greg behind me, I turn me head and glance over my shoulder. But Greg is nowhere to be seen. Instead, a sow with two cubs sits but a few yards away at the water's edge.

Bears fascinate me. For the last several years my work has almost exclusively evolved around them. I have devoted a major part of my time to studying, observing and photograph-ing these magnificent beasts—though usually from much farther away. The immediate re-estab-lishment of a far more comforting and—at least in my eyes—more appropriate distance is at this moment at the very top of my racing mind. Unfortunately, all of my avenues of retreat are blocked except one. The option of swim-ming across to the island, which is still occupied by the young male, ap-peals little to me; it is made even less attractive by the thought of twenty pounds of camera gear dangling around my neck while I try to stay afloat. I am not overly worried about the sow taking the offensive any second now. Obviously, she does not consider me to be a threat; otherwise she hardly would have come this close. Although I don't doubt her placidity in the least, her attitude might change rapidly should she consider her offspring in danger. Her aggression does not have to be directed toward me at all to get me into seri-ous trouble. I may just be in the way.

Unlike myself, the large female, weigh-ing about six hundred pounds, appears to feel no discomfort whatsoever in our mutual proxim-ity. Without so much as sparing me a glance, she turns her back on me and stares out across the wa-ter. A tree stump would have attracted the same attention. By contrast, her ten-months-old cubs seem to share her tran-quility to a much lesser degree. They huddle up against their mother, seeking comfort in physical contact. Their heads move from side to side nervously look-ing around. Occasionally they eye me suspiciously, but their concern is di-rected primarily toward the subadult male on the grassy island.

Suddenly the female raises to her full height. For one short moment she stands motionless on her hind legs at the water's edge. Then she slowly wades out into the river, her eyes fixed on a spot ten yards in front

So it has come about that the distorted image of an animal only vaguely resembling a bear haunts many. Often, the only aspect that does not conflict with reality is the physical appearance. **The rest is a wild mixture of half truths spiced strongly with imagination.**

Bears are only bears, not teddies, but not monsters either.

of her. I take advantage of the opportunity, grab my camera gear and carefully walk passed the cubs. Slowly, I regain my composure as my heart rate calms after reaching the shelter of the trees. Another story for the pub, which sounds good only in retrospect. When I turn around, I see the sow swim back to shore, holding a salmon in her mouth. Her return is ea-gerly awaited by her nois-ily begging progeny.

Some beliefs, regardless of how they contradict all reason, are engraved so deeply into our think-ing, they almost become cultural heritage. So it has come about that the distorted image of an an-imal only vaguely resem-bling a bear haunts many. Often, the only aspect that does not conflict

with reality is the physical appearance. The rest is a wild mixture of half truths spiced strongly with imagination. Brown bears are considered highly unpredictable. And grizzlies, traveling their remote high mountain retreats in the American and Canadian Rockies, stand in total disrepute, considered guilty of indiscriminate manslaughter. A deep gulf separates reality and myth, its span wider the further away from the present-day range of the animal. The yellow press has done its share to keep the fear of bears alive and to add fuel to the flame. An uneventful meeting with no harm done to either party is not worth a single line. Thus the impression is given that the Reaper circles in a holding pattern above every bear-man encounter. If the sow had been the least interested in acting according to her reputation, I would have gotten the opportunity to examine the quality of the local medical facilities quite thoroughly—and this only if I had been very fortunate. The way things went, tattered nerves were the only injury I suffered, and I was richer in knowledge about myself. Even in me, despite knowing better, there still lurks the conditioning of decades, making itself known under "extreme circumstances".

Much too often bears have had to pay with their lives because their inherent curiosity was misinterpreted as aggression. How would I have reacted, if the sow had come even closer and a gun had been in my hands? Fear is a terrible counselor, yet misplaced confidence, carelessness, and contempt are no better. Abandoning the cloak of caution may also bring about fatal consequences. Bears are only bears, not teddies, but not monsters either. They are but impressive denizens of the wildlands, demanding our respect. Dread only changes into respect if understanding replaces ignorance. The unknown is feared. However, our modern industrialized society is plagued by a general alienation from nature. Meanwhile, we feel the urge to re-establish contact with our environment. Bears are tranquilized and radio-collared in order to follow their movements on a computer screen. Yet, to no one's surprise, we still do not seem to transmit on the same wavelength.

Our disturbed relationship with bears is symptomatic for a society that regards the environment foremost as a resource waiting to be exploited—and at that, often just for tourism. It stands in stark contrast to the deference many early cultures showed for bears and in which they hold the animal to this day. In general, in hunter-and-gatherer societies, man regarded all animals as equals endowed

with human capabilities, if not supernatural powers. Wherever bears roamed, they were held in great honor. Due to their varied diet, their ability to walk on their hind legs, and the fact that a skinned bear carcass closely resembles a human body, they were considered the animal equivalent to man—a furry person, a relative, or a messenger and a link between the worlds. For instance, along the coast of Southeast Alaska, the Tlingit who are still in touch with old traditions regard brown bears as half human. The Ojibwa called bears anijinabe, their word for Indian. The Blackfeet term o-kits-kits refers to both the human hand and a bear's paw. And the Inuit believe the animal is able to temporarily slip out of its coat and walk about as man without being recognized. A walrus ivory carving depicts a person and a bear seated back to back. Their bodies merge and become one. The man appears to be singing. Perhaps the bear sings also.

America's native people are not the only ones who honor the bear, as is evidenced by cave paintings in Central Europe. The oldest depictions date back 35,000 years. In Péchialet, in the Dordogne, the images of two men dancing with a bear are carved deeply into a rock wall. When the agrarian society replaced the hunter-gatherer culture, man's attitude and relationship toward the bear saw drastic change. A black-and-white portrayal of the environment evolved as mankind started to plant fields and raise livestock. The flora became divided between useful plants and weeds. Animals that neither served the economy nor contributed to one's edification were categorized as pest and vermin. Classified as "bad" were in particular species that considered domesticated, dull-witted animals as welcome prey or fields as a set table. Thus, the future of bears in the world of mankind was predetermined. They could

only emerge defeated out of any conflict that would inevitably ensue. Worship and adoration turned into dislike, if not outright hatred. Our vision tainted by vile emotions, we began to see predators in the most fiendish colors to create moral justification for their merciless persecution and eradication. The bear hardly would have been bothered by the loss of image. However, he was no match for the destructive ingenuity of mankind, which exhibits its potential to the fullest whenever an obstacles has to be removed or an enemy annihilated. Armed with high-handed righteousness and a sense of civil duty, man hounded bears with dogs, ran arrows and lances through their bodies, destroyed them with poison bait, and blasted them with bullets from muskets, pistols and rifles. Along the American frontier, people like David Crockett and William "Buffalo Bill" Cody were not held in contempt as butchers but instead were

celebrated heroes. Yet humans were not satisfied with simply exterminating the bear. The majestic animal was put on display, imprisoned in cages for the amusement of the public. During the reign of Emperor Nero, four hundred brown bears as well as three hundred lions lost their lives in a single event in a Roman coliseum, massacred by the cavalry.

Despite all our efforts, we haven't been able to drive the brown bear into extinction yet. In total, about 125,000 to 150,000 bears still roam the earth. Most of them live in the vastness of Russia. However, with the demise of the Soviet empire, those populations are in sharp decline. In Western Europe, small numbers are found in Spain, Italy and the Balkans. In Norway and Sweden, a negative population trend was successfully reversed after hitting a low in the 1930s when only 130 animals were left in the wild. Ever since, bear numbers have been in-

creasing in Scandinavia, and today seven hundred individuals again inhabit the forests and tundra in these countries. The total population of brown bears in North America is estimated to be fifty thousand animals, thirty thousand of which live in Alaska. In the United States, the brown bear or grizzly has lost 95 percent of its former range south of the Canadian border. Whereas tens of thousands of grizzlies may have lived in the Lower 48 as recently as 1850, less than one thousand remain today. The days are gone when these impressive beasts still roamed the High Sierra of California, the Cascades of Oregon and the Rocky Mountains of Colorado. Nor is there space for them on the prairie anymore.

Brown bear populations are stable in America today due to stringent hunting regulations and their strict enforcement. Over the last few decades, several areas with high bear density have been put under protection. Some of them became tourist magnets. Although a rat's nest of problems accompanies an increase in the bears' popularity, the development gives rise to hope. As long as places like the Brooks River are not loved to death, either by voluntary or forced restrictions, they provide us with the opportunity to establish a new relationship with these magnificent animals. These natural wonderlands, in which the protection of bears takes precedence over the interests of people, teach us that it is possible to live in harmony with the beast. All that is needed is for people to observe some rules of conduct and show respect for the animal. There can be no doubt that the agencies entrusted with the task of managing these areas have played no small part in the fact that, despite high visitation numbers, no person has come to harm on the Brooks River since the establishment of Katmai National Park. However, to give credit where credit is due, bears, above all, deserve our gratitude for a peaceful co-existence, considering that every year some tourists show shocking behavior and total disregard for the animals.

The salmon the sow brought back to shore is quickly gone. All that remains of the fish are a few bones and the head. Shortly afterwards the cubs give in to tiredness, snuggle up to their mother, and fall asleep. The female has dug herself a belly hole. Soon she also doses off, her nose hidden between her paws. Every once in a while she lifts her head, checking the area. I cast a last glance upon this family idyll, then turn around and start to walk back to camp. The sun will soon drop behind the trees. The cold drains my energies. It is time to prepare dinner and replace spent calories. A while later, in the last light of the day, I stand next to my tent, holding a cup of hot tea in my hands. Alpenglow drapes the mountains across the lake in soft hues of red and pink. Down on the shore, a bear slowly makes his way along the waterline. His long claws dig deep into the soft sand. It is my hope that at the end of all days the tracks of the great brown bear can still be found among the footprints

of the last people on earth. Maybe, if mankind proves capable of sharing the land with the beast, there is hope that we can learn to live peacefully with our fellow man. Above all, it depends on our willingness to show good intent, tolerance and understanding for the needs and idiosyncrasies of others—both man and beast.

Two dark, wet **balls of fur** cling to her so closely that they continuously get between her legs. The new season has brought new joys.

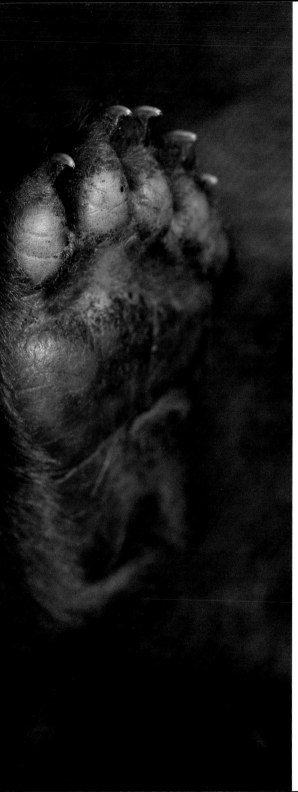

In my head I thank the ingenious mind that gave us synthetic rubber! My raincoat keeps the water out and the sweat in. Better damp and warm than soaking wet and cold. It is a typical day on the Alaska Peninsula in late June. Storm gusts whip the torrential rain into horizontal sheets of water. The heavenly deluge cascades in rivulets from the hood of my jacket—my private waterfall. The wet reality is further pounded into my reluctant mind by the sight of my camera gear wrapped in plastic bags. While morosely contemplating the conditions, I arrive at a conclusion: next year I'll photograph in the Central Australian desert. The mountains on the opposite side of Naknek Lake are only vaguely visible, as if born from a hazy memory. Whitecaps bestow the appearance of an ocean upon the landlocked waters. Today only the very brave and suicidal go out by boat. This is a day unsuitable for any outside activity, a day when fresh air may be considered healthy only with severe reservations. Summers in this northern corner of the globe are basically wonderful: endless days interrupted by short periods of twilight. At the Gulf of Alaska and along the Bering Sea there is only one disadvantage to this part of the cycle of seasons: the drum beat of rain is often heard very loudly. Those in need of excessive sunshine to lighten their spirit, invariably walk on the verge of depression.

The downpour ends as suddenly as it started. Deep blue patches in the sky are lost between windswept shreds of clouds. The slight improvement in atmospheric conditions has a profound effect on my state of mind. My dormant optimism has awakened. After all, I may still get the opportunity to expose some film.

At this moment, the Brooks River is a distant cry from a wildlife photographer's dream. Bears are few and far

Newborn bear cubs are blind, tiny and appear almost naked. From the tip of their noses to the hardly noticeable stump of a tail, they measure just

8 to 9 inches
and weigh
14 to 18 ounces.

Of all the higher mammals, bears give birth to the smallest young in comparison to the size of the mother.

The reward of perseverance: Male bears pursue females in estrus sometimes for a week before she finally loses her fear and yields to him.

between. The salmon season has not yet commenced. Although a few fish have already found their way into the river, any attempt to catch these early arrivals is a waste of time and energy; the meager result does not justify the effort. Thus, the bruins display restraint. Every so often, a bear shows up along the river, puts its head in the water, glances briefly at the void of potential prey below, and then ambles off again. Flowers, grasses, and roots dominate the bears' diet at this time of the year: rich in vitamins, but poor in kilocalories. Based on such food it is quite impossible for the animals to add soft curves again to their gaunt bodies, the result of the past winter. Contrary to popular belief, spring is a time of hardship for bears, a time when they continue to lose weight. Some juvenile or extremely malnourished individuals may even starve to death despite a stomach full of greens. Although plants play a major role in their nourishment — in many areas a bear's diet exceeds eighty percent vegetable — the animal's digestive system, unlike that of ruminants such as cattle and sheep, is unable to brake down cellulose, the structural component of all plant cells. Bears overcome this by being very selective in what they eat. But what choice is there when in spring all food available is rich in cellulose, yet offers little else? Clearly, the bears long for the days of overabundance during the salmon migration. Disappointment is written large across their faces when every river inspection produces the same sobering result.

Wildlife photographers are considered patience incarnate. The term "stubborn" is more accurate. At least I cannot claim for myself the ability to await calmly the unfolding of events. So far, the only thing I have to show for a prolonged water resistance test, lasting several hours, is a pair of wet socks. However, at this very moment my persistence is rewarded. The rain has just stopped, when a bear appears at the edge of the woods a hundred yards upstream, and slowly makes its way through the tall grass toward the river.

It is impossible to observe bears over a period of several years without developing a personal relationship with specific animals. And so it happens that inevitably, sooner or later, individuals are named by those who study them. Although eight months have passed since I have last seen her, I immediately recognize Chowmane. Her slightly concave snub nose is unmistakable.

The first time Chowmane was seen along Brooks River, she was but six months old, weighed about thirty pounds, and was in the company of her mother, Goatee. Since that day, seven years have passed, during which Chowmane has spent every summer and fall along this stream. From the very start, her demeanor toward people has been governed by nonchalance. Mostly she ignored those strange bipeds. Aggressiveness has never been a part of her behavioral repertoire. Cubs learn from their mothers by example, and not even the most importunate fisher-man could ruffle Goatee. When Chowmane finally stood on her own, it appeared she took comfort in the proximity of people over the next few summers. Possibly she felt some sense of protection in their presence. Brooks Camp is closed in the winter. A few years back, when several park employees arrived in May to open up the tourist facilities in preparation for the new season, they were greeted by Chowmane. Much to their consternation, she raced toward them across the still-frozen lake, jumping into the air, showing every sign of exhilaration, and kept coming until she was but a few yards away.

Her temperament has cooled somewhat as she has aged. Meanwhile, she has become a full-grown, independent female, neither avoiding nor seeking the company of humans. Two summers ago, at the age of five, she was traveling the river with her first litter. It became evident quickly that raising offspring is no easy task,

Continued on page 47

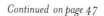

Meanwhile, the cubs have become deeply involved in
a wrestling match
and are oblivious to the fact that their mother is
leaving their side. With obvious delight, they throw
punches and bite each other's neck and shoulders.

To raise her progeny as well as to put on a layer of fat for the winter ahead, a sow with cubs has to consume

20,000 kilocalories per day.

requiring some practice. Chowmane failed miserably as a mother. Her inexperience and an extremely poor salmon run worked against her and her progeny. Chowmane was forced to leave her young to fend for themselves. Otherwise her own survival would have been in jeopardy. Abandoned by their mother, the cubs either starved or fell victim to a predator. Both of her cubs vanished in the fall. Nature is unforgiving. Thin as she was, even Chowmane's prospects looked gloomy. Six months of hibernation lay ahead of her during which a bear loses as much as 30 perecnt of its body weight. And a lac-

tating female may lose as much as 40 percent. But how to put on the layer of fat so desperately needed if the cubs constantly demand their rights? In October of last year, I almost didn't recognize Chowmane. Well-fed and barrel-shaped, she must have doubled her weight in comparison to the fall before, probably turning the scales at more than 600 pounds. However, the honor for the highest gain in weight by a bear is held by a seventeen-year-old female polar bear from the Canadian Arctic. When she was tranquilized and measured in November, she tipped the scale at 218 pounds. The following June she was caught

again. This time, weighing her proved far more difficult because she had filled in tremendously. Now, the scale showed 904 pounds.

Half hidden in the high grass, Chowmane's current maternal status is indiscernible. However, as she reaches the water, there can be no doubt anymore: two dark, wet balls of fur cling to her so closely that they continuously get between her legs. The new season has brought new joys.

Chowmane's maternal blessing does not come as a total surprise. I expected her to have a new litter this year. Her autumnal portliness suggested that much. From a human perspective, the reproductive biology of bears is somewhat unusual. Sexually mature females without dependent young mate in early summer. If the development of the embryo proceeded the way it does in most mammals, the cubs would first see the dim light of the den during the worst imaginable part of the year:

early winter. To avoid such a uniquely unfavorable timing for birth, it appears logical for bears to simply delay courtship and coupling until the season is further advanced. However, hibernation puts an end to such speculations. The animals would need to scour their home range for a willing partner in November, a time when most bears have already retreated to their dens. But nature always finds a way. In all mammals, including bears, the ovum is fertilized within a few hours of mating. Upon fertilization, the zygote divides until it becomes a spherical sac one to two millimeters in diameter, called a blastocyst. From this stage on, the pattern of development in bears differs from the "standard". Instead of the blastocyst being implanted in the uterus, all development ceases and a quiescent stage ensues. This phenomenon is known to science as "embryonic diapause", or as "delayed implantation". The pregnancy awakens from its physiological slumber when the female goes into hibernation in late fall. Hormonal changes reactivate the blastocyst. While the exact details are not known in bears, probably the hormones prolactin and estrogen are involved. If the female was able to accumulate sufficient fat reserves during the course of the summer, a placenta develops, the blastocyst implants, and the embryo's development proceeds to completion. In late January or early February, the cubs, usually between one and three in number, are born in the security of the den. But if the sow was unable to store enough fat to sustain the energy demands of herself as well as her young until spring, the pregnancy aborts and the blastocyst dissolves.

Now, a mid-winter date of birth holds problems as well. However, hibernation determines every aspect of the development of the fetus, from conception to bearing the young, allowing no later time of delivery.

Newborn bear cubs are blind, tiny and appear almost naked. From the tip of their noses to the hardly noticeable stump of a tail, they measure but eight to nine inches and weigh around fourteen to eighteen ounces. Of all the higher mammals, bears give birth to the smallest young in comparison with the size of the mother. A female may weigh three to five hundred times as much as the newborn cub. If applied to man, this would translate into a birth weight of a human infant of three to five ounces. The delivery would certainly be easier and less painful, but even our best pediatricians, assisted in their efforts by the most sophisticated technology modern medicine has to offer, would be hard pushed to save such a premature baby; and if the baby survives, it often struggles with multiple problems. For bears, on the other hand, birth in an early devel-

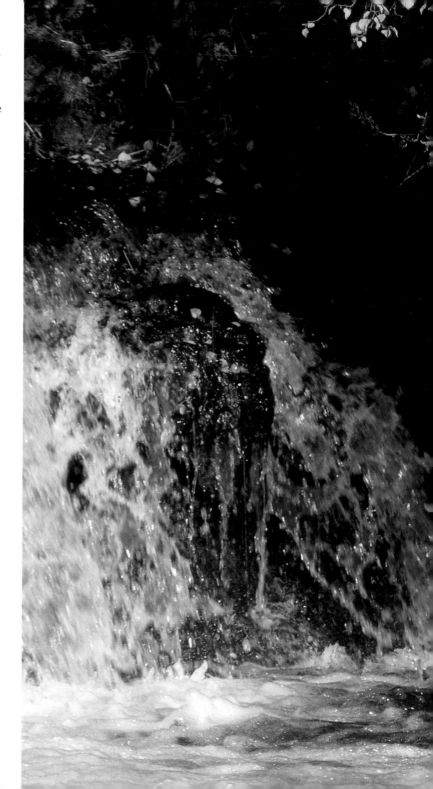

48

Every so often, a bear shows up along the river, puts its head in the water, glances briefly at the lack of potential prey below, and then ambles off again.

opmental stage is just the way it is.

A fasting mammal meets its nutritional requirements from body reserves. The same is true during hibernation. The bears do not wake up to feed on stored foods. As bears gestate during this period of winter sleep, in order for the cubs to have the entire summer and fall to grow and fatten up, a problem arises: the energy demands on a mammal during pregnancy are huge. The body fat content of an expecting female can be sixty percent upon entering her den. Yet, by the time she leaves her winter retreat with her new litter six months or more later, her weight will have dropped by as much as half. In most areas her condition will continue to deteriorate for

at least another month before feeding conditions improve. If the cubs were only marginally bigger than what they are, reproductive success would decrease as most mothers would have to abandon their offspring to avoid starvation. If the females would carry their young to what we consider full term, she would emerge from hibernation unable to move her own body. Hence, the gestation is shortened, and the cubs are born in a premature stage.

Like all mammals, the newborn cubs are raised on milk, which is extremely rich in bears. In grizzlies, average fat content in the milk is 22-24 percent to fuel the high burning metabolic furnace of the cubs. The protein content is between 11-15 percent to provide the essential amino acids for muscle development. In the next few months the cubs grow rapidly. By May, when they start to explore the world outside their den, they have become boisterous small bears

weighing between ten and fifteen pounds.

Chowmane's cubs fit this description perfectly. They are lively fellows, studying attentively the surrounding area from between her legs. Still wet from the downpour a little earlier, they look like they have just fallen out of a washing machine. Their dark fur is completely tousled. Chowmane awards me a short glance and then sits down at the water's edge. A few minutes later she rises again and wades out into the river. Meanwhile, the cubs have become deeply involved in a wrestling match and are oblivious to the fact that their mother is leaving their side. With obvious delight, they throw punches and bite each other's neck and shoulders. Then, all of a sudden, the fighting ends. The surroundings regain shape and with it the realization that an important element of their world is amiss. Although their mother is only thirty yards away, they start to

display signs of distress. Fidgety, they stand up, look in all directions and utter a short, hoarse bark. Without hesitation, Chowmane heads back to shore. It is apparent that the cubs have difficulty identifying their mother visually, as Chowmane's approach does not arouse the expected enthusiastic response. Instead, a hint of panic descends upon her offspring. Frightened, they run into the tall grass, seeking shelter there. Seconds later their heads pop up above the green blades a few yards away. They peer toward Chowmane, still uncertain whether she represents danger or protection. Not until she huffs and pops her jaw are they certain of her identity, and finally they relax and return to the shore. Another crisis in their young lives is over.

Animals that raise their offspring in relative isolation often display a limited ability to identify their own progeny. The same is also obviously true for the capability of bear cubs to recognize their mother. Cases of cub swapping have been observed repeatedly along salmon streams. Primarily this happens when several family groups with young of equal age fish the same part of the river, and the cubs mingle. With many bears around, the cubs are agitated, nervous and occasionally get confused to the extent that they follow the wrong female upon her departure from the river. Most often the young bears are reunited with their biological mother within a few hours. Occasionally, however, they remain permanently with the foster family. In one instance, a sow was observed with cubs of different ages, one of which was most certainly not her own. In general,

the foster mother appears to have little problem with the new addition to her family or the swapping of family members as long as the strange cub keeps calm. Should the adoptee become nervous, timidly bellowing for its true mother, acceptance on the part of the foster parent may turn into lethal intolerance. Upon observing bears for a long time, one truth emerges clearly: there are no absolutes in the realm of animal behavior.

Chowmane's visit to the river was of short duration. Reunited, the family disappears shortly afterward into the nearby forest. In the absence of fish, there is no point in staying. I have not taken a single picture. But Chowmane will return. In the days ahead, I will get plenty of opportunity to capture her on film. To raise her progeny, as well as to put on a layer of fat for the winter ahead, a sow with cubs has to consume twenty thousand kilocalories per day. Thus, a female can ill afford to ignore a rich resource such as Brooks River during the salmon migration. For me, just seeing an old acquaintance again was worth my wait in the rain. I only hope her attempt to raise offspring will be crowned with success this time.

Ten days later, early in the morning, a dead bear cub was found half buried on the shore of Naknek Lake, one paw sticking out of the sand. During the course of the night, the little fellow had fallen prey to another bear. It was one of Chowmane's cubs. In the weeks following the incident, nobody saw Chowmane along the banks of the Brooks River. When she reappeared, she was alone. Some wishes are made in vain.

Top: From its vantage point high above, one of Chowmane's cubs scrutinizes its surroundings. In case of danger, sows often send their offspring up to the safety of these lofty timber retreats. Due to their mass, adult bears are inept climbers at best; and large males are simply unable to ascend into the crown of trees.

Right: Fortune did not smile upon Chowmane's third litter either. Toward the end of August, she disappeared, abandoning her three cubs to their own devices. From then on, they searched the shores of the Brooks River alone despite being devoid of maternal protection. To sleep, they bedded themselves near the base of large trees in order to be able to take refuge up high if threatened.

On the opposite side of the stream appears
a bear.

Shadowy, as if sketched against a white background, he stands in the tall grass. The fog muffles all sound creating the impression that the animal is moving in a shroud of silence.

The sun is a yellow disk low above the eastern horizon. Haze hangs over the river in wavering filaments, with mist veiling its shores. Apart from the occasional yammering call of a gull and the gentle murmur of the water, the land lies enfolded in quietness. A bear appears on the opposite side of the stream. Shadowy, as if sketched against a white background, he stands in the tall grass. The fog muffles all sound, creating the impression that the animal is moving in a shroud of silence.

These peaceful morning hours are the high point of my day. While people in camp still stretch luxuriously inside their tents, enjoying the pleasant warmth of their sleeping bags, bear traffic along the river is heavy, amounting to a bruin rush hour. Now, in mid-July, the salmon have shown up in huge schools in the Brooks River. In these first hours of light, many bears fish the stream, including animals that at any other time of the day stay away to avoid humans. After the short night, they have awakened hungry, and the prospect of a rich breakfast buffet draws them to the water.

About six hundred yards upstream from the river's mouth, beyond an oxbow that redirects the water's might, the current has dug deep into a little hill, carving a cutbank out of the small rise. On top of it, a few yards above the water, I have taken up my photographic watch.

The bear on the opposite bank vanishes in the mist like an apparition. My field of vision extends slowly. A little way upstream I notice a sow with two cubs. From the distance, I am uncertain of her identity. However, as the family group draws closer, I recognize Ester and her young. In the world of bears, where bigger is definitely better, she is positioned high up in the hierarchy. Weighing in prime condition about 900 pounds, Ester is the largest female along the Brooks River. Although in size she is still no match for the huge males, even they usually give her a wide berth when she has cubs.

Ester's offspring see their second summer. Since last year, they have grown enormously. The scrawny brats of the previous summer have changed into adventurous, roly-poly hooligans full of mischief. In a wrestling match, even the strongest of men would take a terrible beating. Last fall when a nine-month-old cub was weighed, the scale showed 125 pounds. These fellows have left that mark far behind.

Ester scrutinizes the river briefly to make sure the stream is hers alone. Then, with her cubs in tow, she unhurriedly follows the shore downstream. But within a few dilatory steps the procession grinds to a halt again. Ester stands up and looks out across the stream. She stares intensely at the shallow water in front of her before falling back on all fours. After a glance over

The scrawny brats of the summer before have changed into **adventurous, roly-poly hooligans** full of mischief.

59

her shoulder, she walks on for five more yards. Another wary look in both directions, then she wades into the river, leaving the cubs on shore. Hitherto, Ester's gait has revealed no purpose. She ambled along as if enjoying a morning stroll to greet the new day. Now, however, her stance communicates tension and intent. For several seconds she remains motionless. Then the morning idyll is lost in a blur of motion. And to the onlooker it becomes apparent that some attributes we consider characteristic of bears are inspired by wishful thinking rather than fact. The proverbial leisureliness and complacency of bears is mostly myth. Bears can run at a pace of up to thirty-five miles per hour. Even a world-class athlete would be left in the dust in a hundred-yard dash.

With a sudden burst of speed, Ester sprints out into the middle of the river, leaps forward with her paws stretched out, and vanishes with a loud splash behind a sheet of water. The river around her becomes alive. Salmon jump haphazardly everywhere, trying to escape. The water seems to boil. Ester has landed amid a shoal of fish. Her energetic fishing style has produced results. Her powerful paws pin a salmon to the rocky river bottom. With a quick motion she grabs it with her teeth and carries it back to shore.

Ester's cubs have paid rapt attention to her efforts. Then, as realization strikes that their mother will not return empty-handed, they race toward her excitedly. Wailing at the top of their lungs, they take up position in front of her. Judging by their actions, one is tempted to believe starvation is imminent and death can only be cheated out of what is rightfully his by means of this very salmon. However, Ester is unwilling to surrender the first salmon of the day. Without paying any heed to their plea, she begins to eat the fish.

Continued on page 67

Hitherto, Ester's gait has revealed no purpose. She ambled along as if enjoying a morning stroll to greet the new day. Now, however, her stance communicates tension and intent. For several seconds she remains motionless.

Then th

morning idyll is lost in a blur of motion.

With a sudden burst of speed, Ester sprints out into the middle of the river, leaps forward with her paws stretched out, and vanishes with a loud splash behind a sheet of water.

The river around her becomes alive. Salmon jump haphazardly everywhere, trying to escape.

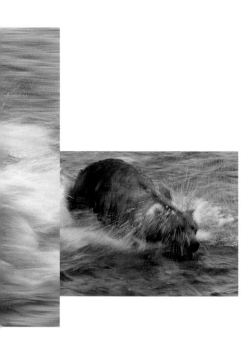

If she is lucky — and the fish not so lucky —

the bear's head reappears
seconds later with a
4,000 kilocalorie
snack in its mouth.

As reward for his insolence,
she clouts her cheeky cub with a hard slap.

Wailing at the top of their lungs, they take up position in front of her. Judging by their actions, one is tempted to believe starvation is imminent and death can only be cheated out of what is rightfully his by means of this very salmon.

Still, ignoring a double dose of 160 pounds of all-consuming appetite is easier said than done. Announcing its frustration and protesting loudly, the more courageous of the two cubs attempts to pull the fish away from under the mother's nose. Ester feels obliged to resort to a paw-founded educational method. As reward for his insolence, she clouts her cheeky cub with a hard slap. However, where one alone fails, teamwork may lead to success. Rascal Number Two takes advantage of this second of inattention and steals the

fish. Pursued by his associate in crime, he races off in full gallop with the stolen goods.

Ester watches them, making no effort to fetch back the salmon. In her eyes, the issue is settled as soon as her offspring gained control over the fish. She turns away, once again giving her attention to the river. For Ester's cubs, the joy over the loot is brief, the green-eyed monster of sibling rivalry lurking in the mind of both. A heated argument flares up that is only settled when one cub retreats into the tall grass holding the tail section in his mouth while the other takes off with the head.

It is quite the norm among bear cubs to aggressively demand food. The young are almost never totally full and constantly ask for more with vehemence. Furthermore, it is nothing out of the ordinary for them to get their hide tanned. At times it may even be dangerous to harass your mother as evidenced by an incidence that happened two years ago. A sow lost her patience over the incessant whining of her offspring, and bit him in the backside, unintentionally hitting an artery. The cub bled to death.

This intermezzo along Brooks River has lasted a little longer than a minute, and ends with Ester standing up to her shoulders in the river, again exploring her fishing prospects. Forty yards away, hidden in the tall grass, her cubs are preoccupied with the task of gulping down the fish to the last scale. Once again, the river is a place of peace. But wherever bears congregate in great numbers, trouble is never far away.

At this moment, I notice a bear in the water downstream from Ester. As he becomes aware of her, he gets out of the river, attempting to bypass her along the shore. Time and again he casts Ester a cautious glance, all the while oblivious to the fact that the grass behind him shelters her progeny. Thus far, he has escaped Ester's attention. Her interest is still directed toward the river and the dinners contained therein. Yet, the safety of her cubs is never far from a mother's mind. When Ester turns around to check on her young, the strange bear has moved between her and her offspring. In such situations, ignorance is not accepted as an excuse. Although unknowingly and without intent, the animal has broken one of the fundamental laws of bear society: never step between a mother bear and her young! Without hesitation, Ester charges, plowing through the water toward her unwitting opponent. He appears confused about what has caused such a radical response and tries to take refuge in flight, speeding off upstream for a few yards. But then he stops and turns around. It is better to take the charge head-on than to be mowed down from behind. Also, one's backside is endowed with virtually no communicative abilities. Ester, like a hellcat trapped in the body of a bear, storms closer, throwing herself into the fray without slowing down. To absorb the impact, her ad-

versary rises up slightly. Ester's front paws swing against the shoulder of the other bear. Then both face each other, their mouths agape. The roar of the assaulted bear can be heard a mile away where the racket awakens park visitors from their dreams. For several tense seconds both animals freeze. Then Ester and her opponent slowly retreat backwards. Twenty yards away, the cubs stand next to each other in the grass, observing the conflict like disturbed visitors in an open-air theatre.

During such confrontations I am always uneasy. One can never be sure how the bear under attack will react. It has happened more than once that the bear under pursuit headed straight for the nearest person. These habituated animals have learned that most bears will keep clear of those two-legged, smelly beings. Consequently, there is some protection to be gained — and thus physical contact with the other bear avoided

— by seeking shelter behind somebody's back. Understandably, the enthusiasm of the person involved is somewhat subdued. To know a bear is right behind you is unsettling enough. To have a second coming toward you at a dead run is bound to cause worse nightmares than any Steven King novel ever could.

Although the attacked bear might disagree,

from Ester's point of view her aggressive behavior is justified. The river is a dangerous place for cubs. One-third of the young never live to see their first birthday, 60 percent never grow to adulthood. Some succumb to diseases, others starve to death, and many fall victim to other bears.

Several hypotheses have been put forward about this phenomenon. Many biologist seem to

Never step between a mother bear and her young:

Without hesitating,
Ester charges.

subscribe to the theory that a male increases his chances to reproduce by such infanticidal behavior. The progeny of the competition is eliminated, and many a time a sow will go into estrous again within a few weeks of losing her cubs, giving the male the opportunity to pass on his own genetic material.

Observations in the wild, however, contradict this line of thought or at least raise doubts that are hard to dispel. In addition, in my opinion, this explanation appears to be borne from the desire in natural sciences to force all of nature into a linear structure of cause and effect. But often the matter is much more complex, and the reasons for one and the same outcome may differ if conditions vary.

Infanticide can only further the reproductive success of a male if he can be certain of his parental status in regard to the youngster involved. If he kills a cub he sired himself, his behavior would backfire on him. His chances of passing on his genes to the next generation would decrease instead of increase. Now, bears are not much into monogamy. Males mate with several females. Nor do sows practice fidelity. Determination of fatherhood based simply on sexual partners is thus impossible. In addition, under stress, even bear mothers, as cases of adoption and cub swapping demonstrate, have difficulty telling apart their own offspring from strange cubs, both visually and by smell. Hence, it can be ruled out that a male would be able to do so. Furthermore, since the sow does not become sexual receptive for a number of weeks after losing her litter, there is no direct feedback, and any one of a number of males may reap the sexual benefits of the situation.

Genetic aspects provide additional cause for doubt. If infanticide, in fact, represented a reproductive advantage, such a behavioral strategy would be written into the genetic code and consequently would be widespread and almost

universally used. Most if not all males should then display interest in ridding the population off cubs they themselves have not fathered. However, this is not the case. Most mortalities are simply the result of unfortunate circumstances. As a rule, it is just a matter of being in the wrong place at the wrong time. Also, each bear has its own character. Many boars ignore or avoid sows with cubs. Then there are those that would be considered maladjusted or asocial in human society. Females are well aware of these individuals with attitudes. They flee from them and show fear of them when they have cubs. They even evade them when they have no young to care for. It appears unlikely that those males would be favored by the sows and more successful than other boars in planting their seed as soon as the female becomes sexually receptive again.

In addition, the victims are not restricted to cubs. Independent subadults have been slain in confrontations with large boars as well. Such killings have no bearing on the reproductive success of the aggressor. However, I believe the most important counterargument is the fact that death does not come by the claws and jaws of males alone. Females are also involved in the killing of cubs.

In my opinion, infanticide is a side effect of bears' tendency to interact aggressively with members of their own kind. The animals are solitary by nature. Their survival depends on their ability to defend food resources against competition and to utilize every available source of nourishment. Congregations of bears, such as those along salmon streams, are the exception, and restricted to times when food is available in over-abundance. The innate opportunism and the aggressive predisposition offer an explanation for the vast majority of cases of infanticide. Only this line of argument provides an answer to the question of why males

**Finally,
Ester gives in.**

**Half sitting,
half lying on her back,
she keeps watch in all
directions ...**

...while her two cubs work her teats, humming constantly.

would go to the extreme of killing a female that is defending her progeny. Just last year, two cubs were orphaned. Their mother simply disappeared one day, presumably after sustaining fatal injuries in a fight with a dominant male. In addition, it offers an explanation for the observation that boars, in an act of cannibalism, will feed on the bodies of their victims occasionally. Still, one should refrain from lumping all incidences of infanticide together. Bears are extremely adaptable animals with a rich behavioral repertoire. Every bear is an individual in its own right, with its own character and own peculiarities. Individual animals react differently to the same environmental stimulus. Depending on the animal's emotional state, a similar situation may even trigger an opposite response in one and the same bear. This does not mean that bears are unpredictable, but rather that they are intelligent creatures, not machines.

In view of the risks involved, one is tempted to question the wisdom of raising cubs along the river. Some bears, in fact, do not. However, the physical demands on the sow are extremely high while she is nursing. To sustain the rapid growth of her cubs, the sow is in need of copious amounts of food, and the salmon run provides just that. Thus the decision to raise cubs along the river or not, involves gauging the risks against the benefits.

The recent events have shaken Ester's offspring badly. They remain nervous even after the family is reunited. Above the murmur of the water, I can hear their purring with which they make known their wish to be nursed. Both try to reach Ester's nipples. Evidently, even among bears, nursing has a pacifying effect. However, Ester is unwilling to yield to her cubs' request. Where they are, they could be surprised much too easily. She walks downstream a few yards, but her cubs don't let up. Finally, Ester gives in. Half sitting, half lying on her back, she keeps watch in all directions while her two cubs work her teats, humming constantly. Their world is happy once again. For a short while, peace has returned to the river.

Salmon

erupt from the churning waters

in an attempt to clear the barrier. In many cases, the trajectory is flawed by serious miscalculation.

Halfway along its short journey from lake to lake, the Brooks River tumbles across a five-foot ledge of rock that spans the width of the stream — and the river suddenly reveals its hidden force in a thundering wall of water. For the salmon, the falls represent a surmountable barrier; despite its modest size, the cascades disturb their ranks. Where before the independent motions of each individual fish quite miraculously joined to become part of the harmony of the school, now underwater chaos reigns. Salmon erupt from the churning waters in an attempt to clear the barrier. In many cases, the trajectory is flawed by serious miscalculation. Instead of entering the calm of the river beyond the cascades, fish plunge back down amidst the whirls and are thrown back to the foot of the falls. Soon salmon congregate there, scale to scale, a swirling mass of thousands of fish, packed so tightly their bodies seem to merge into one.

During the salmon migration, Brooks Falls is a place were dreams of gluttony come true for the bears of the area. The fishing styles of the animals vary. Some position themselves at the lip of the falls, their paws firmly placed on the rock ledge beneath the water's surface, and await, mouth agape, the leap of a salmon. Brooks Falls is one of the few places on earth where nature literally throws the next meal into the expectant mouth of a bear. At the peak of the salmon run, more than four hundred fish attempt to leap the cataract each minute. With nature's bounty at its richest, it does not take long until a bear returns to shore with a fish in his possession. Others take their position below the falls, trying to take advantage of the brief confusion after a badly timed vault. The most popular spot of all is a place about midstream where the plunging river creates a large whirlpool.

Even when all other fishing locations fail, the vortex still frequently produces a salmon dinner. Sitting on its haunches, the head just above the water, a bear marks time until a fish touches its front legs, then lunges in the turbulent water after the object of its desire. If the bruin is lucky—and the fish not so lucky—the bear's head reappears with a four-thousand-kilocalorie snack in its mouth. However, more often than not, the fish gets away.

In the early stages of

Some position themselves at the lip of the falls, and await, mouth agape, the leap of a salmon. Brooks Falls is one of the few places where nature literally throws the next meal into the mouth of a bear.

the salmon run, bears consume almost the entirety of their catch; apart from mandible, upper jaw and gill plates, little remains for the gulls to fight over. Later, after fishing success has become commonplace, they are more selective. Some large males land as many as fifty salmon per day, but when food is overabundant, they ingest only those parts that offer the most calories per bite. Because a gram of fat yields twice the calories of a gram of protein, the choice bits for a bear are those richest in fat: skin, brain, and caviar. The red meat they leave behind. Weight gain is the primary objective of a bear's diet. Under ideal conditions, their daily rations amount to more than twenty thousand kilocalories. With intake at such a gargantuan level, a bear is able to add four-and-a-half pounds to his weight in a twenty-four-hour period. Weight Watchers would never be able to enlist new members among bears. At times, large males may stand in the middle of a large pile of salmon carcasses. From the distance, the skinned fish look as though they have been cleaned and prepared for a barbecue. Yet, although nature may be lavish, it is never wasteful. Downstream, subadults and sows with cubs feed on the scraps that fall from the breakfast, lunch or dinner table of the dominant boars. Bald eagles, ravens, magpies and gulls steal what is left.

Above all, Brooks Falls is the domain of the large males. Many females, concerned about the safety of their cubs, shun the cascades when these giants of bear society are present. Next to fully grown males, sows appear modest in size. On average, they go to scale at two-thirds the weight of large boars. This discrepancy in size and mass makes it more difficult for females to control the risk every non-family member represents. Body size as a gender characteristic of adult bears is the evolutionary result

of strong competition for mating privileges. Going strictly by figures on paper, there appears to be no shortage in sexual partners. In bear populations, males and females are represented in about equal numbers. However, simple math-

ematics are deceiving. As a rule, a female introduces her offspring to the secrets of a bear's life for a period of two to three years, protecting them until they are old enough to fend for themselves. Thus, roughly only one-third of sows show any

interest in amorous matters in any given year. So it happens that several males compete for the sympathies of one female.

In the last few days, Brooks Falls has been at its busiest. As many as ten bears simultaneously

shared the rich fishing grounds of the cataract. Salmon lay in the water like a dark cloud. Four days ago, fishermen working the mouth of Naknek River pulled their nets. The Depart-ment of Fish & Game closed their fishing

window to give more salmon the opportunity to reach their spawning grounds. As a result, forty-eight hours later, the Brooks River was crowded with fish. Yesterday evening, a subadult bear sat at the top of the falls like a rock in a salmon surf. Stoically, he endured the ceaseless assaults launched by the fish, hardly moving to ward them off. Salmon collided in mid-air with the animal, crashing against his nose and ears. Mostly he showed no reaction apart from closing his eyes or turning his head aside. A few times he waved his paw

Choice bits:
skin, brain, and caviar.
The red meat they leave behind.

as if trying to shoo away annoying flies. People are not the only ones who find that a full stomach drains vitality. This young bear had gorged himself on salmon to the max. With no room left to consume any additional fish he appeared to be fascinated by this spectacle of nature, rather then interested in food. A salmon crash-landed between his legs. All of a sudden, without the expenditure of any effort on his part, he held a wriggling fish in his paws. For a short moment he looked at it. Then he let it go, and the fish fell back into the river. Live and let live.

A heavenly deluge finally drove me from the river. All night long the rain played a lullaby on the fly of my tent. Not until the early hours of morning did the much-longed-for final chord fade away. Now, heavy dew, glazing the vegetation, is the only evidence of last night's downpour. Unfortunately, not only the rain but also the fish have said their farewells. The salmon come in waves, accentuated by the long arm of the fishing industry. Downstream, along Bristol Bay, the nets are back in the turbid waters. Some salmon always get through, but the great masses are stopped when obstacles with a fine mesh block their way. The windows during which fishermen can pursue their quarry are small and vary from year to year; the authorities watch that salmon migrate up every drainage system in sufficient numbers. Still, man's efforts have an impact. The bears quickly realize that fishing will produce little result today. Thus the absence of salmon is met by general inactivity on part of the bruins. Weather and light are excellent, but in terms of photographic subjects: zilch.

In the humid morning air, my breath hangs like a faint white cloud in front of my mouth before dissipating. Shivering lightly, I sit crouched next to my camera, exercising patience. As a

80

Continued on page 86

Salmon collided in mid-air with the animal, crashing against his nose and ears.

Mostly he showed no reaction apart from closing his eyes or turning his head aside. A few times he waved his paw as if trying to shoo away annoying flies.

As many as ten bears
simultaneously
shared the rich
fishing grounds
of the cataract.

**Salmon lay
in the water like
a dark cloud.**

83

wildlife biologist and photographer, I had plenty of opportunity to perfect this essential virtue. Today, reality belies the reputation of Brooks Falls; the cascades lie deserted in the pale morning light. Around 10 o'clock, a large male pays a visit, only to leave again soon after for the lack of a prospective meal. As the hours advance, boredom and the chill of the day slowly start to get the better of me. As visions of hot coffee appear in front of my eyes, I decide to pack up. I am about to leave my observation point when a huge male emerges from the dense brush. Scanning the surrounding area, he slowly wades out into the water, making his way over to the whirlpool. A few days back, we had christened him Rambo, a name that seemed to fit perfectly because of his forceful attitude and well-executed way of winning respect by flexing his muscles. This year, Rambo is king at Brooks Falls. Even individuals

such as Panda, who the year before enjoyed the view from the top in local hierarchy, keep a respectful distance.

But what good does brute strength do if the salmon make themselves scarce. Two hours later, Rambo is still sitting in the frigid water, biding his time, without having caught a single fish. Some bears are extremely patient, and this large fellow apparently decided to set an example for perseverance.

Watching a bear, even if it is Rambo, that is doing nothing except sitting up to its neck in water, is interesting for only a short while. Over time, concentration slips, the mind wanders off, and the bear loses my undivided attention. The secret of wildlife photography is the synchronization of the activity of the actors in front of the camera with those of the person behind it. Unfortunately, photographers are no strangers to Murphy's Law: "Whatever can go wrong, will go wrong,

and at the worst possible time". The most dramatic events unfailingly occur when you least expect them, when you are ill-prepared, and when you are as far as possible from having your camera at the ready. Just like right now.

Suddenly, the serenity of the day is replaced by a deafening roar and a wild commotion. Unnoticed by me and—more significantly—by Rambo, another male has approached under cover of a small island in the river. No bear ever remains river sovereign uncontested; evidently the newcomer has sneaked up on Rambo, intending to seize the moment and take advantage of a surprise attack to move up in hierarchy. However, the attacker has been too optimistic in evaluating the situation. He quickly loses his edge as Rambo explodes from the water as if ejected, crashing full speed into the flank of the other bear and bowling him over. Now on top of the assailant, the advantage

is all Rambo's; from the looks of it, serious, if not fatal, injury appears inevitable. With mouth agape and paws flying, Rambo bears down on his challenger. Yet, just short of tearing into his opponent, he stops. For a few seconds, time seems to stand still. Motionless, the two boars remain locked in combat. Then they part, and warily the defeated bear moves off in a slow, stiff-legged gait, carrying a deep gash on his foreleg. Nor has the victor escaped uninjured. A gaping cut three inches

long adorns Rambo's forehead. Numerous scars on his neck attest to previous confrontations with similar outcome. However, Rambo is oblivious to such minor "scratches". He watches his rival walk off, then moves over to a stand of alders. With powerful blows from his front legs, he prunes a few of the little trees. Branches lie between his paws. Then he rises up on his hind legs and rubs his back against the trees, urinating at the same time.

All the while, the

action below is matched by my desperate attempt to pull my camera out of the bag. The entire event lasted no more than twenty seconds. By the time I have the camera ready to shoot, I am able to document only the victor's display of dominance. After mutilating two more trees, Rambo, too, walks off. Once again all is quite at Brooks Falls. Every couple of minutes, a solitary salmon becomes airborne, reentering the water a second later.

I am torn between

the frustration of not being able to capture this episode on film and the delight over being privileged to witness the event. Conflicts fought with such grave determination are rare, especially now in mid-July, when the salmon season is already in full swing. Serious arguments occur mostly during the mating season from mid-May to mid-June and in the first weeks along Brooks River, when the hierarchy is not yet clearly established. Even then, most confronta-

its front legs, then lunges in the turbulent water after the object of its desire.

tions are restricted to threatening gestures and signals of submission. Physical contact is the exception, and if it occurs, mostly limited to the exchange of a few left and right hooks. As a rule, the resulting scratches leave both animals none the worse for wear physically; the bears mostly ignore the small injuries. On the other hand, emotional bruises incurred by the trouncing are frequently very noticeable. Some years back, when Bullet was not yet fully grown,

he was unable to claim prime fishing spots at the falls. In confrontations, he invariably came off second. Chased off by a dominant boar, he wandered downstream. The way he moved and his stance clearly revealed the seething unrest within. Aggression bottled up inside needs an outlet. Right then he regularly ran into humans fishing along the banks. In the mood he was in, Bullet was unwilling to give way and surrender the river once again. Instead, to enforce the fact that

these fishing sites were his by right of greater strength, he resorted to intimidation — usually successfully. In those years, it was not uncommon to watch a disturbed angler race into the ranger's office, where, struggling for breath and gesticulating wildly, he described in detail how minutes before he had narrowly escaped a huge brown bear, and this only by the most fortuitous of circumstances.

Yet the risk of coming to harm in such an encounter is small if one

doesn't aggravate the situation. The behavior of bears is aimed at preventing physical confrontation in order to minimize the risk of injury. Now, bears do not live in herds or packs. By nature, they are solitary animals. Outside the mating season, adult individuals interact with each other very little socially. Mostly the animals avoid each other. Because the evolution of anatomical features is steered by purpose, bears have only limited capabilities when it comes to

Continued on page 94

Suddenly, the
serenity of the day
is replaced
by a deafening
roar.

For a few seconds, time appears to stand still.
Motionless, the two boars remain
locked in combat.

Rising up to his full, imposing height of over nine feet, Rambo rubs his back against the remains of small trees, displaying his dominance. Numerous scars on his neck attest to previous confrontations with similar outcome.

body language. There is no need for communication that goes beyond the basics. Thus, a bear's ability to form facial expressions is rudimentary; the requisite muscles are poorly developed. The tail, which clearly conveys the emotional state of mind in dogs and wolves, is but a short stump and unsuited to giving a visual signal. The ears are small and no better at conveying a message. Due to these physical limitations, the communication of bears is more straightforward than is that of many other animals. It lacks nuances, and intervening steps are often skipped. Hence, the animals react to threat with little warning, which has given rise to the widespread belief that bears are highly unpredictable. But they are, by no means, more unpredictable than many other mammals. Bears do give signals. Often, however, they are misinterpreted or not recognized as such. For instance, a yawning bear is far from being bored

or tired. Instead, a yawn signals stress and unease — and that it's time for the human observer to retreat from the immediate vicinity of the bear. Similarly, foaming at the mouth is not a sign of rabies, but rather another step towards fight or flight. Such signals are often given when the so-called magic circle of a bear, a personal space of individual diameter, is violated. If theses signs of warning and distress are ignored and the trespasser does not withdraw, the bear will attempt to reestablish sovereignty of its magical circle, either by departing himself or by removing the transgressor.

Most encounters between bears end before the animals ever get into close contact. Body size determines dominance. Generally, serious confrontations develop only between individuals of similar bulk, height and weight. Only maternal females break this rule. Because of their aggressiveness, they take positions high up in

hierarchy, only surpassed by adult males.

If two individuals get into a confrontation, it is usually a nonviolent standoff with the interaction restricted to threat displays until one bear shows submission and slowly retreats. Taking refuge in flight almost always triggers a wild chase. Hence, there can be but one piece of advice to the slow-footed human who finds himself in a comparable situation: never, by threat of possibly severe injury, show a bear a pair of heels, even if one's heart temporarily sinks to some lower part of the anatomy. Attacks are mostly fake charges. Normally, bears do not view people as prey, competition, or adversaries. Where they have become habituated to the colorfully clothed two-legged beings that share their environment, where they don't consider them a threat and have never learned to associate people with food, maulings are almost nonexistent. However, to regard them with a blasé

attitude invites disaster. Respect and prudence are prerequisites for safe travel in bear country. Although accustomed to people, bears in places such as Brooks Camp are still wild. They differ from bears in other areas, not so much that they are less aggressive, but rather less shy. Just as bears everywhere else, these animals still maintain a magical circle; it is only smaller. Thus the risk of surprising the animal, and forcing it to react, is reduced.

I leave the falls shortly after Rambo. Making noise as I go so as not to surprise a resting bear, I slowly follow a narrow trail meandering through the high grass that lines the river. About half a mile downstream, I notice Bullet on a gravel bank. In front of him lies a freshly caught salmon. Bullet lifts his head upon becoming aware of me, throws me a disinterested glance, and then returns his attention to his catch. Some things change over time.

I leave the falls
shortly after Rambo and slowly follow a narrow trail meandering through the high grass lining the banks of the river.

The crash of splintering wood pierces my dreams and rouses me from a sound sleep.

The crash of splintering wood pierces my dreams, rousing me from a sound sleep. Instantly, I am wide awake. Nothing speeds up the circulatory system like a dose of adrenaline. Seconds before, my heart had been chugging along unhurriedly, now my pulse is racing. A quick glance at my watch provides me with no information. The position of the hands cannot be determined; their turquoise fluorescence had dimmed to blackness during the night.

My fingers search for the flashlight. In contrast to the clutter in my room of childhood days, everything has its place in the tent. If only my mother had guessed that I could keep order if necessary… The beam of light cuts through the dark like a knife. 12:30 A.M. As if knowledge of the time mattered and would help me in the least.

I hear loud crashing, as if a door is being ripped from its hinges and thrown to the ground. I sit in my tent, desperately pon-

dering my options. It is early October. I am the only person still staying in Brooks Camp. During the day, a few park maintenance people are working to board up the cabins and buildings to protect them against vandalizing bears and the worst of winter.

However, they are housed a mile and a half away on the opposite side of the river. I can yell until I am blue in the face; nobody will hear me. Paying them a midnight visit is out of the question. The pontoon bridge is broken down into segments and pulled ashore, and I

don't have a canoe. There is no way I am going to walk upstream in almost complete darkness to a spot where I might cross the river in waders without flooding them. I get the matches out and light the lantern. If a bear shows interest in my tent, maybe the light will deter

him from entering; the thin material of the fly most certainly will not.

I open the tent door and glance outside. The futility of any attempt to assess the situation visually is instantly apparent. I might as well stare at a black velvet cloth. I cannot see a thing.

With the eyes blind, the hearing sharpens. Faint sounds thunder like canon fire. Distances lose dimension. The source of the racket appears to be but a few steps away, yet it must be at least twenty yards. That is how far it is to the food cache. To prevent bears from developing a taste for preserved food, chocolate bars, and other camp delicacies, the park service erected a small but strong, windowless wooden building. Three latches lock the heavy door. Judging by the din, the bear is wasting no time pushing back the bolts. Instead, he appears to be tearing down the entire shed.

There is good reason for the security concerns of the park's administration. Between 1900 and 1980 some nineteen people were fatally mauled by brown bears in North America's national parks. There are records of another twenty-two deaths elsewhere in Alaska. Most of these incidents could have been avoided if

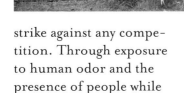

the people had acted properly and if better precautions had been taken. The causes for the majority of fatal human-bear encounters fall into one of two categories: either a female that saw her offspring endangered was involved — the family was often surprised —, or the bears had learned to supplement their diet with human garbage or with camping supplies. As soon as the quest for food has produced a digestible result, bears act like prospectors who have come across a vein of gold. Nothing can keep them from returning, and they defend their

strike against any competition. Through exposure to human odor and the presence of people while acquiring sustenance, the bears lose their fear of man. Even without considering people prey, the animals may become dangerous. As soon as they have discovered that edibles may be found in tents, backpacks, cabins, or generally in the vicinity of man, they will revisit these place. Occasionally, should the opportunity present itself, they will enter human dwellings, paying no heed to whether they are occupied or not. Those who try to defend their sleeping quarters or property have a serious problem on their hands unless they are able to support their claims with pistol, shotgun, or rifle power. Bears are notoriously bad at sharing. They protect their food source jealously against their own kind. But man's physique is substantially more fragile than a bear's; thus he is much more vulnerable to physical abuse in the form of bites or powerful blows by long-clawed paws.

Due to the popularity of the Brooks River, prudence is a necessity. As of yet, in Brooks Camp no visitor has ever been injured by a bear since the establishment of Katmai National Park. Although in the past some bears, especially individuals representing the animal equivalent of teenagers, occasionally shredded tents, they usually indulged in this pastime during daylight hours when the owners were absent. Curiosity and high spirits were the incentives. These colorful objects, which even bounce back when pushed down, were a temptation too powerful to resist for the average juvenile bruin.

They have never found food inside the tents. In fact, edibles probably weren't at the top of their minds when they went through people's temporary residences. In general, bears thoroughly inspect all unknown objects in their environment. In experiments in zoos, bears investigated curios such as toys in their enclosures more intensely and for a longer time than primates. Some individuals even developed complex games. This exploratory behavior is part of the animals' survival strategy, a characteristic that has a direct bearing on the success of the bear as a species; close inspection of its surroundings may reveal a food source thus far unexploited. The innate curiosity of bears combined with their sometimes rollicking character also finds expression in behavior that is unrelated to the acquisition of nourishment, such as play.

Bears of all ages play. The younger they are, the more intensively they do so. Dominant boars only rarely condescend to frolic about with another bear. Cubs in their first year of life, on the other hand, almost continuously occupy themselves with the subjects and objects of their surroundings. Siblings tussle with each other. In the case of an only cub, the mother serves as a surrogate playmate. The physical activity promotes healthy bone growth. Also, by engaging in games of tug and war, by tussling, and by wrestling, the cubs practice survival skills. By playing with other bears, social bonds are reinforced and social behavior is refined. This last aspect is probably the reason behind the friendly bouts between adult animals. However, such wrestling matches fought with a lack of seriousness may also have an end in themselves. Upon observing the animals it is difficult not to believe that they sometimes play for no other reason than sheer enjoyment.

As a rule, in Katmai during June and July only cubs and some juveniles indulge in play. Occasionally a maternal female gets included in the game, but in general adult bears are too preoccupied with either mating or restoring depleted fat reserve to surrender to the lightness of being.

At the end of July, after the salmon have passed through, the bears leave the river. The fish

Continued on page 106

They have never found food inside the tents. In fact, edibles probably weren't at the top of their minds when they went through people's temporary residences.

Bears thoroughly inspect all unknown objects in their environment.

Subadult bears search the beach of Naknek Lake for salmon washed ashore. Whether these individuals are large yearling cubs, or two-year-olds still under the protection of their mother, or whether they are independent juveniles cannot be ascertained by body size.

Lucy may well be called the terror of the Brooks River.

travel up Brooks Lake to reach the feeder streams, where they deposit their eggs in shallow depressions in the gravel bed of the creeks. The bears follow the salmon in order to continue their feeding orgy. Not until the leaves are turning do they return to the Brooks River. Individuals easily identifiable a month earlier, are now almost unrecognizable. Their winter coats have grown back. Even before, the animals were most impressive. In September, however, they are truly colossal after having gained their fall weight. A thick layer of fat covers their frame and adds softening curves to their figure. Now, as the question of survival during the long period of hibernation in the following winter is answered, there is plenty of time to enjoy life. Due to the associated photographic opportunities, I appreciate this fact greatly. However, the park's administration harbors no such sentiments. The bears are now in their destructive prime. Wherever their claws and teeth find hold, the animal set to work. Their damaging enthusiasm unchecked, they take apart almost everything, from outhouses to metal garbage containers set in concrete. Bolting, nailing or screwing something down, provides little protection. The bolts, nails, and screws may be the only things left in place when the bears are done. Last fall, two bored five-year-old juvenile delinquents discovered that doors cannot withstand the impact of their mass. Standing up, a short push with their front legs saw the door flying inward, complete with lock and hinges. Inside, much of interest presented itself. Sometimes there were only plain government furnishings. On one occasion, however, they forced entry into the laundry room, which also serves as storage space for books for the park employee rec room. The bears checked out the light reading. Books of all sorts, from murder mysteries to romance novels, lay strewn about. After having discovered little of interest among the soft-cover volumes available, their curiosity shifted to the appliances. The top cover of the washing machine was bent open as if someone had gone to work on it with metal shears, pliers, and hammer in order to add a second access to the drum. By the time park service saw itself compelled to protect the buildings against the ruinous inquisitiveness of the bears with an electric fence, the two bruin burglars had broken into thirty cabins. But a few thousand volts dampen even the most exuberant bruin's enthusiasm.

The two delinquents were always easily chased away. Like two juveniles aware of their wrongdoing, they fled immediately when people appeared on the scene of the crime — only to return as soon as the spoilsports were gone again. The problem multiplies if cubs still under

maternal care start to display destructive behavior, especially if the mother is Lucy.

Lucy may well be called the terror of the Brooks River. Some even regard her as their private nemesis. I, for my part, am perfectly happy spending my days along the stream without ever laying eyes on her. This is particularly true in years when Lucy is accompanied by cubs. In contrast to most other sows, Lucy feels uncomfortable in the proximity of man. Many females, such as Chowmane for instance, do not regard people as a threat to their progeny. Quite the contrary. It appears some even see an advantage in being close to humans, as many big boars shy away from the immediate vicinity of man. Thus, a person, unintentionally, may represent protection for their young. Lucy, on the other hand, for whatever reason, is distrustful of people. Possibly her negative opinion of man is based on bad experience. Conceivably, while roaming the land, she may have crossed the park's boundary, encountering people with a less-than-sympathetic attitude toward bears. If this is the case, the question arises: why does Lucy continue to visit the Brooks River. Salmon streams abound in this part of the world. But then, Lucy's aggressiveness may simply be part of her character. Based on her behavior toward other bears, nobody would feel tempted to consider her the "bruinification" of friendliness either.

Lucy as a problem bear is a cyclic occurrence. In years when she is without cubs, she visits the Brooks River only occasionally, keeping her distance from people. Every three or four years, she shows up along the river with a new litter. The first summer passes almost without incident. The cubs stay close to their mother. Confrontations with people are rare. However, in the second year, reports of close encounters begin to come in. As her young

They approach

people out of curiosity,

to determine who or what they are. They inspect buildings to test them for structural soundness. Always, they live in the certainty that, should trouble arise, their mother is nearby to defend and support them.

get older, they grow bolder, exploring their environment in partial independence, often determining the family's route of travel. Lucy's role in the family frequently resembles that of a maternal appendage. Her stubborn offspring are responsible for most of the conflicts the family gets into. Out of curiosity, they approach people to determine who or what they are. They inspect buildings to test them for structural soundness. Always, they live in the certainty that, should trouble arise, their mother is nearby to defend and support them. Lucy follows her offspring at a distance. Often she remains unnoticed, and her cubs are considered subadults in their first year on their own. However, any attempt to keep the juveniles at a distance or to prevent them from ripping the door jamb off a cabin, reveals their true status. Much to the unpleasant surprise of the person involved, who these young bears are is instantly beyond doubt as one suddenly faces a furious maternal female named Lucy. As the year advances, Lucy becomes increasingly nervous and aggressive. One fall, after Brooks Camp had already been closed down for the year, the park's management felt pressed to resort to rubber bullets to divert Lucy's *enfant terribles* from their path of destruction. The projectiles are relatively harmless; for a few days, the animals sport a painful bruise where the bullet hit, serving as a medium-term reminder of the unpleasant encounter. Yet, what had worked so well with previous problem bears, failed in Lucy's case. Instead of keeping her young away from the danger zone, she started to attack the marksman. From the point of view of the bear, this was a reasonable reaction. Quite understandably, the person involved saw it differently. It is almost a miracle that nobody got hurt. This episode emphasizes again that it pays to know the bears one wants to capture on film. As a photographic model, Lucy is unquestionably uniquely unsuited. One fact is emphatically called to mind: generalizations do not apply to an individual. Although bears represent no more than a small risk to personal safety as long as all rules of conduct in the wild are observed, there are some bears that are better avoided just as there are malicious people, vicious dogs and kicking horses. Both excessive confidence in the animals and unfounded fear can entail catastrophic consequences for man and animal alike.

The racket in front of my tent continues unabated. If the noise is any indication, there cannot be much left standing of the food cache. Over the last few days, I have had great difficulty keeping bears out of camp.

Until recently, I was not alone. A few other photographers had pitched their tent near mine. The naiveté of some people is beyond comprehension to me. Despite being told of the possible consequences, these colleagues had the truly brilliant idea of preparing all their meals with fresh groceries such as eggs, cheese, and bacon. Admittedly, at present, the bears are living on a dietary cloud nine, overindulging in a salmon gluttony, and their interest in an alternative source of nourishment is limited. Thus, under the prevailing circumstances, an odorous menu does not draw my full-hearted objection, although I do not consider such an aromatic cuisine advisable by any means. However, one is truly tempting fate when the dirty dishes are cleaned on the bushes nearby instead of in the lake, and when leftovers are thrown into the fire pit, instead of being properly disposed of, in the assumption that mice and magpies are faster than bears at getting to them. One morning I discovered that overnight the fire pit had been transformed into a three-feet-deep crater. Without question, this was not the work of any rodent or bird. In expectation of uninvited guests, I moved camp. If possible, I wanted to wait a few years before investing into a new tent. When the black sheep of the camping community finally flew out, they left behind a tarp, white gas for the stove, and their trash. I could have done quite happily without the latter. Within a short time, the garbage developed an impressively rich bouquet. The sense of smell of a bear is comparable to that of a dog. Faint scents and fragrances undetectable to us, represent to bears invisible, yet very clear, signs directing the animal to the source of odor. As the pungent stink irritated even my sorry excuse of a sense of smell, there was little wonder that bears ran through camp all day long, there noses testing the air, trying to establish where

this most promising aroma originated. I made preparations to bring the garbage to the incinerator building at the Ranger Station, although my idea of fun most certainly does not include carrying a bag of trash through the woods. The transport was planned for tomorrow morning — evidently too late.

Again came the sound of breaking wood. Occasionally, wildlife photography is blessed with unforgettable moments. This one certainly qualifies as such

Although in the past some bears, especially individuals representing the animal equivalent of teenagers, occasionally shredded tents, they usually indulged in this pastime during daylight hours when the owners were absent.

as well, although not in a positive sense. With a feeling of uneasiness, I recall having seen Lucy with her cubs close to camp yesterday. Finally, at about two o'clock in the morning, the din starts to abate. Yet, sleep is slow in coming. I abstain from counting sheep as they would only turn into bears, leaving me more wakeful than before.

At some point, I must have dozed off. Around eight o'clock, I rouse from sleep. Dawn is breaking. The wind rustles the trees. Waves gently wash against the shore. No other sound disturbs the peacefulness of the morning. I climb out of my sleeping bag, put my clothes on, and step out of the tent to inspect the destruction. To my surprise, the food cache is still standing. Even the door is in place. At eye level, two large paw prints smile at me. More cover the backside of the building. Down low, where the plywood boards meet the ground, a bear has tried unsuccessfully to pry the wall open. Apparently all attempts were thwarted by a lack of implicit desire to get inside. Upon rounding the cache, I find the source of last nights pandemonium. Several one-gallon can- isters of white gas and a few propane bottles are strewn about on the ground. All show teeth marks. In the middle of everything lies a totally destroyed box, almost unrecognizable as such, which once was used for fuel storage. Imagination had played a trick on me. Nevertheless, I'll remove the trash today. My tat- tered nerves are in need of rest. One night like the last is enough.

Snow is falling.

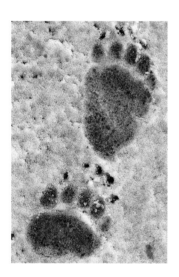

Snow is falling. The forest stands in silence — a shadowy backdrop partly obscured by the flurries. Utter stillness envelopes the forces of nature. The charm of the weather lies in its contradictions, communicating a homey, cozy feeling. The flakes swirl in the wind, dance above the yellow grass, play around the gnarly trunks of the trees, and finally descend upon the frozen ground. A tenuous veneer cloaks the cold, pale reality of late fall. Brown leaves and dark earth vanish under an isolating, immaculate blanket. The winter sends white greetings from the northwest.

I follow the Brooks River downstream, the heavy camera bag flung over my shoulder and the tripod in my hand. The bank is fringed with ice. The calendar shows October 21. The last few weeks, the land had lain under the sway of bitter cold, the temperatures dipping below zero degrees Fahrenheit at night. But now the wind carries on its wings not only snow, but also moderate temperatures. At conditions just a few degrees below freezing, I feel like spending my time in Alaska's banana belt. There can be no doubt: my stay in this part of the world has lasted far too long already. I start to overheat in my jacket, and pull down the zipper.

Over the last several days, fewer and fewer bears have traveled the river. The animals are leaving; the fall exodus has commenced. Only the very core of the bruin population of the area still searches the stream for spawned-out salmon that sink to the bottom or get washed ashore. These gifts of the river's current lack much of their former nutrition. Salmon fast upon entering freshwater, living off their fat reserves. When those are depleted, the energy requirements of the body are met through the breakdown of muscle tissue until the fish ultimately, unavoidably, perishes. Thus, in fall, the calorie content of a

The forest stands in silence — a shadowy backdrop partly obscured by the flurries. Utter stillness envelopes the forces of nature. The charm of the weather lies in its contradictions.

salmon is at best half of what it was in July. These questionable autumn delicacies require a strong stomach and are very much an acquired taste. At least to unaccustomed palates, the late-season flavor of "red fish" leaves much to be desired. Bears are strangers to the subtleties of nature's cuisine. They do not scorn such unsightly prey as long as the equation "calories obtained minus energy expended" arrives at a positive result.

Near its mouth, where the Brooks River loses itself in the immensity of Naknek Lake, I notice a bear in the middle of the stream. Only the head is visible. From a distance, the animal could be mistaken for a walrus gone astray from its ocean home. The bear rises up in the water, takes a deep breath, puts his head on his chest, and submerges in one smooth motion. The huge, well-padded backside is visible for a fleeting moment, then the entire animal is gone. There is absolutely no question about its identity: the bear in the water is Diver. Like no other bruin, he perfected the technique of underwater fishing as if the watery habitat were his by nature. According to the laws of physics, he should float at the surface like a cork. Excursions into the realm of fish should be close to impossible. Apparently, a good technique does wonders. Ten seconds later, Diver reappears in my field of vision, snorting loudly. Again he breathes in deeply, subjecting the river bottom to another thorough inspection. Diver submerges three times, reappearing each time with no digestible prey in his mouth. However, on the fourth try, Diver breaks the surface with a salmon locked between his teeth. Many times, he gulps down his catch right there and then, riding the deep waters like a living buoy kept afloat by thick layers of fat on his paunch and hips. This time, however, he swims to shore and drags himself halfway out of the water. There, just a few yards away from me, he sinks down on his front legs and starts to eat the fish.

Diver is the Methuselah among the bears of the Brooks River. Rumors have grown up around his age. The record among bruins

Continued on page 135

Ten seconds later, Diver reappears in my field of vision, snorting loudly.

Many bears search for food in the water, but like no other, Diver perfected the technique of underwater fishing as if the watery habitat were his by nature.

Only the very core of the
bruin population of the area
still searches the stream for
spawned-out salmon that sink to
the bottom or get washed ashore.

for the most years lived is held by a captive female that departed her zoo life at the biblical age (for bears) of forty-five years. In terms of seasons seen, Diver cannot compete with her. He has probably watched thirty summers go by. His best days have long since passed. Until a few years ago, he was the seldom-challenged sovereign at Brooks Falls. Few bears dared to dispute his lofty position. Today, he avoids all confrontations, having slipped far in hierarchy. Yet, despite his loss in authority and the associated inability to defend the best fishing spots against younger, more dominant boars, Diver has been able to keep his weight. He is as voluminous as ever, presumably thanks to his exceptional fishing tech-

nique. It appears that, by means of diving for his quarry, he has secured for himself a food source not used by any other large boar, which in turn may be the reason for his longevity.

Nevertheless, the ravages of old age have left their mark. His breathing is heavy. Plagued by arthritis, he avoids extensive travel on land. In his struggle with gravity, he gratefully accepts the assistance of water, buoyancy lending him a helping hand while he is drifting along with the current or wading slowly upstream. From his head to the tip of his long claws, Diver is rarely seen. But even partly submerged, he is a most impressive figure, being a truly immense animal. In the course of the

summer, he adds more than 300 pounds of fat to his leviathan frame. By the end of fall, he easily tips the scale at over one thousand pounds, his huge belly almost dragging on the ground.

If man were to abandon himself to a cycle of fasting and feasting, the consequences would be serious, if not fatal. Yet, what amounts for a human being to a dietary avenue toward suicide, is for bears a necessity in order to survive, hibernation demanding its toll. Also, in contrast to man, excessive obesity for bears is much less of a health problem.

In Western society, its ideals of beauty determined by spindly, anorexic models, an entire industry has developed around the size and

distribution of fatty tissue. Man, unlike bears, does not depend on extensive fat reserves in order to survive. On the contrary; the love handles of a human male, the result of fat deposited in the abdominal cavity, are associated with a range of medical complications, including an increased risk of heart attack. Women, on the other hand, store the majority of fat subcutaneously on the hip and thighs, a pattern far more beneficial for general health. In bears, the distribution of fat in both sexes is similar to the pattern in women: their extensive fat reserves are located primarily under the skin. In addition to the medical advantages, this distribution also carries the benefit of provid-

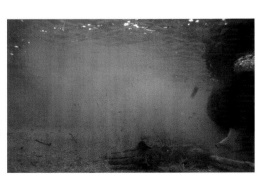

In fall, the
calorie content
of a salmon is
at best half
of what it
was in July.

ing a layer of thermal insulation several inches thick; because of this, a healthy adult bear is in no danger of becoming hypothermic even under extremely adverse conditions. The animals spend the winter in hibernation because of food shortage. Temperatures far below freezing pose little problem. Frequently, Diver does not even bother to retire to the comforts of a dry day bed. Instead he dozes at the water's edge, his head resting on shore, while his belly, hind legs, and hips are still submerged in the river. His compact, rotund body encased in massive subcutaneous fat deposits is impervious to the chill even when water temperatures lie only a few degrees above freezing. His fur, on the other hand, contributes little to thermal insulation when wet, although ten thousand hairs share a square inch of skin in the fall. Yet, comparatively speaking, the winter coat of a bear is still rather flimsy. At the densest spot, the fur of sea otters is composed of up to one million individual hairs per square inch, as the animals rely entirely on their fur to maintain their body temperature.

After consuming the fish, Diver slides back into the water as elegantly as a beached whale. One salmon is certainly not a complete dinner to him, and dessert may be found drifting in the river. Alaska harbors the richest salmon runs in the world. Eight hundred thousand tons of salmon are heaved annually aboard fishing vessels along North America's west coast. A few hundredweight of those left in the waters by the fishermen are pulled from their natural habitat by Diver after the salmon have migrated up the river. In summer, at the onset of the salmon run, he gobbles down as much as 60 pounds of fish per day. Meanwhile, his appetite is finally somewhat appeased; there is an end even to his physical capacity. At the moment,

his food intake serves but one purpose: to keep his weight. To accumulate additional pounds of fat is unnecessary if not counterproductive. In a few weeks, he'll climb the surrounding hills to excavate a den on a north-facing slope. Protected against a sudden mid-winter thaw, this will be his home until mid-April. Diver belongs to the rearguard in regard to this temporary retreat from active life. The first to leave for their winter dens are pregnant females and sows with cubs, followed by subadults. The last to bed themselves down for the long sleep ahead are the dominant males. The bears reappear in spring in reverse order: first the large boars, last females with a new litter. The driving force behind this sequential departure and return is the shortage of food in late fall and early spring. In these border months, nature offers frighteningly few things rich in nutrients that bears can digest. Consequently,

competition for the little available is extremely high. Thus maternal females wait until conditions improve before leaving their den with their progeny, else they would put their offspring at risk.

Diver is but a few minutes in the water when the current serves the next course. At the sight of the fish, the thought of dinner is pushed far from my mind and the feeling of hunger is buried deep under mild disgust. Obviously the salmon had been dead for some time. I am surprised the fish is not falling apart at the slightest touch. Although not opposed to epicurean pleasures, in his feeding habits Diver resembles a walking garbage can. He appears to live according to the maxim: what matters is not taste, just edibility.

Unhurriedly, Diver relishes the questionable joys of his palate. Much to the relief of my nerves, haste is almost unknown to him. In his vicinity, bear photography is a peaceful, relaxing line of work. He is the only dominant boar displaying tolerance toward people instead of avoiding them. Sometimes, he spends his nights in the grass not far from the tents. His snor-

Compared to marmots or ground squirrels, the energy consumption of bears during the months spent asleep is astronomically high.

Bears spend as much as sixty percent of their lives in deep sleep, only to reappear after hibernation as if they have just undergone a slimming treatment

ing keeps me awake and other bears at distance — a fair arrangement with which I can live happily.

In the deceptive assumption that I am somewhat protected against other bears in the shadow of his presence, I drop my guard. So it happens that I become aware of the new arrival only as he already stands on the opposite shore. A large boar has approached the river's edge. For a moment, he watches Diver. Then, noticing me, he huffs nervously. Obviously, in his realm of experience thus far people have played a minor role at best. A feeling of uneasiness washes over me. There is something unusual and unsettling about this animal. His build is odd. The front legs look normal and appear strong due to the long fur but his head is extremely angular, and his upper body is slender like that of an oversized greyhound, instead of barrel shaped. When he turns his side toward me, I realize to

my horror that he is but a walking skeleton. The spine looks as if it were a foreign object sitting atop the rest of his body. Every vertebra is discernible. The hipbones protrude as if laid free by a sculptor. He stands high in the shoulder; in his prime, he would equal Diver in mass. Now, he is only a scraggy shadow of his former self. Reduced from its formerly impressive bulk to a skinny assemblage of skin, bones, and tendons, the animal is driven on only by the will to survive. The last meal must have been several weeks ago. An ugly, gaping wound extends from his hip almost down to his heel. Although the healing process must have been going on for some weeks already, scar tissue has not yet closed the laceration. There can be no doubt about the reason for the pitiable physical condition: he got the worst of it in a confrontation with another bear. In early September, wind and current washed a dead moose up on the

shore of Naknek Lake. Within a couple of days, the carcass became a popular meeting spot for the bruin residents of the greater area. Frequently, serious fighting broke out between bears over this unexpected red meat bonanza. Apparently, this individual was among the losers and, to make matters worse, withdrew too late.

My calm composure evaporates without a trace, and apprehension takes its place. The implications of the situation are easy to grasp. In its present condition, the bear cannot survive the winter ahead. The body temperature of true hibernators such as marmots or ground squirrels chills to within a few degrees of freezing and may even dip below the freezing point. Their heart reaches only one to two percent of its summertime performance. Hence, the bodily reserves burned during the cold part of the year are reasonably small. By comparison, the energy consump-

The last meal must have been several weeks ago. An ugly, gaping wound extends from his hip almost down to his heel.

tion of bears during the months spent asleep are astronomically high. The body temperature drops only six to sixteen degrees Fahrenheit. The pulse slows from fifty beats per minute to about ten. The entire rate of metabolism is cut by half, but a far cry from a near standstill. Hence, the animals lose more than one-third of their body weight while they are lost to the world in prolonged sleep. However, to regard bears as inferior hibernators based on these facts would be a total misconception. The development of the fetus depends on an increased metabolic rate. But it is exactly this higher energy consumption that means almost certain death for the injured male. He is in desperate need of nourishment, which, this late in the year, is in short supply.

Hibernation as it occurs in bears is physiologically impossible for humans, regardless of whether they are lean and mean or in the shape of a Sumo wrestler. Energy supply and consumption is not the real issue. Due to the fact that bodily functions are slowed but not dramatically reduced, a number of physiological problems arise that are far more difficult to solve than any matters related to fuelling the metabolism.

No living being is ever a finished product, but instead is continuously remodeled according to current physical stress. Even after growing up, our muscles and bones do not remain the same throughout our adult life. In response to the workload imposed on them, muscle tissue is either built up or reduced. Bones are strengthened, or they thin out and weaken. A bedridden person suffers from muscular atrophy within a short time. Due to weightlessness, the bones of astronauts become fragile during lengthy flights in space. Yet bears stay curled up inside their small dens for months on end without moving. They spend as much as sixty per-cent of their lives in deep sleep, only to reappear after hibernation as if they have just undergone a slimming treatment, but apart from that, are in perfect health. Bear are able to maintain bone and muscle mass in absence of any physical strain by recycling metabolic waste. How, is not known thus far.

This physiological feat has made bears popular research subjects in human medicine. The results will hopefully provide new medication and treatment for diseases such as osteoporosis and severe kidney failure. And the substance that produces in bears the metabolic changes resulting in a lower heart rate and drop in body temperature — dubbed Hibernation Induction Trigger (HIT) — may prove a milestone in organ transplants. Due to tissue deterioration, donor organs are beyond usefulness within sixteen hours, and that only if utmost care is taken. As much as twenty percent of donor organs have to be discarded before they ever reach the operating room. However, if the donor organs are perfused with HIT, the survival time increases almost threefold.

The recognition of bears in modern medicine is a product of the recent past. Yet in traditional Oriental medicine, the bear has played an important role for many centuries, with some bizarre side issues. During the 1988 Olympic Games in Seoul, the Korean government had thirty live Asiatic black bears flown in from Thailand to feed to its athletes in the believe that the meat of the bears would enhance their performance. In Japan, a cup of bear paw soup brings top prices. The watery broth is reputed to confer general well-being and health.

Even more sought after than bear paws is the animal's gall bladder. Dried and ground into a fine powder, the gall bladder sells on the markets of the Far East for over fifteen hundred

144

Continued on page 148

dollars per ounce. The lucrative traffic in bear parts has developed into an illegal industry. There are always some who will plunder their natural heritage if a handsome profit can be made.

In 1985, an Air India Boeing 747 coming from Canada exploded in mid-air and crashed, killing all 329 passengers. In the cargo compartment were two suitcases filled with the gall bladders of approximately a thousand black bears. In the Far East, the shipment would have had a street value of a million dollars.

In China, the gall bladder of a bear has been highly valued in traditional medicine for more than a thousand years. It was and still is the treatment of choice for jaundice, abdominal pain and distention—all symptoms caused by liver and bile duct diseases, and in particular, gallstones. One is easily tempted to banish claims of the healing powers of gall bladders into the realm of fable. However, research has revealed that the old Chinese were right a millennium ago. Gall bladder tea works. Bear bile contains a substance, called ursodeoxycholic acid (UDCA), which dissolves certain kinds of gallstones without causing substantial side effects. Today, UDCA is produced synthetically. Used in hospitals, it is available as a prescription drug. The demand for bear gall bladders, however, has not slackened due to these advances in pharmaceuticals, as Far Easterners credit the authentic product with higher potency.

The bear's reputation has benefited greatly from these recent discoveries of modern medicine. Their amazing biology may help to save human life or at least may improve life. However, sight of the injured bear sends my thoughts on different paths. Compassion for the male is pushed to the back of my mind by the realization that desperate animals are capable of desperate deeds. As a rule, bears are immensely obese in fall. Their temperament fluctuates between lethargy and playfulness. There is no need to search aggressively for food. This individual, though, is forced to act. I have never seen a bear in such dire straits.

The injured boar slowly follows the river downstream. Every few steps he halts to throw

me a sideways glance, then walks on. My efforts evolve entirely around keeping Diver between us. Diver pays little attention to the new arrival; in the water, he has nothing to fear. A hundred yards downstream, the large male crosses the river. The situation starts to give me the jitters. I feel increasingly uncomfortable. Doing my best not to convey the impression of flight, I walk over to the edge of the woods. The spruce trees and birches are too small to climb, but somehow I feel sheltered partly hidden from view. Diver still sits calmly in midstream, devoting himself to his fish meal. As the strange boar disappears for a few moments behind a line of bushes, I decide to take advantage of the opportunity to head back to camp. The time has arrived to test whether my radio equipment actually works. In all these years, I never had to put it to use. I just hope I reach Lynn. He is supposed to pick me up in three days. However, in view of the present situation, an orderly escape appears more than justified. It is debatable whether or not this bear represents a real threat. The animal is hard to assess. It is basically impossible to predict what he will do. But why take an unnecessary risk? The situation would be different, if I had company. But even healthy bears sometimes act pushy toward a lone person.

Three hours later, I hear a distant droning, and shortly afterwards Lynn's plane appears in the sky. Late in the afternoon, after getting airborne, Lynn circles one last time above the river. Near its mouth, I recognize Diver in the water. Without him, the Brooks River could never be the same to me. I have not seen the injured boar again, nor have I ever heard what happened to it.

Bear Facts

The Mating Game

The mating season of brown bears extends from May until early July. Although the majority of bears search for a mate within this period of time, some bruins are occasionally observed much later indulging in the game of love. On the Alaska Peninsula, the record is held by two bears that were seen deeply involved in matters of procreation on August 10. Females that lose their litter early in the year are often in estrous again within several weeks of the tragic event. In the case of unusually late breeding activities, it appears likely that the female roamed the region until recently in the company of offspring.

In bear populations, both genders are represented in about equal numbers. As the females introduce their offspring into the secrets of a bear's life for several years, roughly only one-third of the sows are favorably disposed to the overtures of a male. This statistical imbalance results in high competition among males for mating privileges, which in turn has had its impact on the evolution of bears; adult, dominant males are up to twice the size of females, due to the fact that larger boars have greater success in passing on their genetic material to the next generation.

Although the mating season covers several months, sows are in estrous for only about three weeks. They allow a male to mount during just three to four days at the peak of the estrus cycle. Because the animals, for the most part, lead a solitary existence and congregate in a small area only at times when food is available in overabundance, they face a problem in finding a potential mate at the right time. Hence, bears — dominant boars in particular — travel far across their home ranges during the breeding season. To detect a female in heat, a male trusts primarily his nose. Metabolites of sex hormones are eliminated from the body with the urine. By means of his exceptionally acute sense of smell, a boar is able to determine the receptiveness of a female by sniffing the soil and grass where she urinated, walked, or slept. Nose close to the ground, he unwaveringly follows a promising scent trail for miles. At first, this strong interest on part of a male appears to disturb the female. She tries to evade him, as the much larger boar is potentially dangerous to her. Often the unequal pair is observed for several days as they cross meadows, amble through brush, and travel along streams at an unvarying distance. In time, the female allows the boar to come closer. However, it may take as much as a week before she loses her fear and becomes approachable. The animals soon graze, play, and rest in close proximity. After several days of this intimate togetherness, the female finally permits the boar to mount, copulation usually lasting about forty-five minutes.

Ovulation in mammals occurs either spontaneously without any external trigger such as happens in humans, or is induced by the male such as happens in bears.

Spontaneous ovulation carries the risk that the ovum may die before conception is achieved. The chance that no breeding partner is encountered at the time of ovulation or soon after is small in animals living in herds or family groups. This is not the case in bears, which, as a rule, spend much of their adult life in voluntary separation from their fellow bruins. Thus, to guarantee that a fertile egg is available at the time of copulation, ovulation occurs only upon appropriate mechanical stimulation. A long copulation time and a penis bone called "baculum" are characteristic for mammals that are induced ovulators. In a large male brown bear, the baculum is slightly longer than a pen and twice as thick.

Brown bears usually have several cubs per litter, two or three as a rule. Occasionally, a sow may even give birth to four young. The known record is six cubs. However, such a large family is about as rear as naturally conceived quintuplets in humans. As the cubs are not identical offspring and as each ovulation produces but one ovum, several copulations are required to produce and fertilize the eggs. Consequently, the bears most often remain inseparable for three to four days, copulating on and off. Then the female loses interest in such close contact, appears to grow uncomfortable in the proximity of the male, and wanders away. The boar uses his regained independence to search for further prospective mates.

On the Alaska Peninsula, such an uncomplicated, comparatively peaceful courtship and mating is the exception rather than the rule. On average, there are two bears per square mile of land along the Katmai coast. In June, at the peak of the mating season, the bears congregate on the coastal sedge flats and along salmon streams to feed. Along rivers, where the fishing is excellent, the concentration of bears is even higher. In such crowded conditions, boars are forced to defend their breeding privileges against rivals. Smaller individuals give way to dominant males, which may copulate with four or five, if not more, different females in the course of the breeding season. In confrontations over the right to mate, boars get injured. Gaping lacerations on head, shoulders, and front legs as well as fractured jaws and broken canine teeth attest to the seriousness with which the battles are fought. The high concentration of bears along salmon streams also results in females mating with several males, a situation that primarily arises when a

subordinate male is chased off by a dominant boar. As bears are induced ovulators, it thus may happen that individual cubs of one litter have different fathers.

Gestation, Birth, and Raising Cubs

After mating in early summer, the fertilized egg begins to divide until it is a spherical sac 1-2 mm in diameter, known as a blastocyst. However, implantation of the embryo into the uterus wall does not immediately occur. Instead, development ceases. The blastocyst finally implants into the wall of the uterus in November, after the female has entered the den and is in hibernation. This phenomenon is called delayed implantation or embryonic diapause. If the female was able to build up large fat depots over the summer, the development of the embryo proceeds to completion, and in late January or early February the cubs are born in the security of the den. However, should the fat reserves of the sow be insufficient to sustain both her and her young until spring, the pregnancy is terminated. A surge of estrogen probably reactivates the blastocyst. The hormone prolactin may be necessary to facilitate implantation of the embryo.

Bears are by no means the only animals in which embryonic diapause occurs.

Delayed implantation has been described in about a hundred mammal species. The list contains numerous members of the weasel family including the wolverine, ermine and American marten. Similar quiescent stages in the development of the embryo re typical for kangaroos.

Delayed implantation of the blastocyst prevents the birth of bear cubs in fall at the onset of the cold time of year. As an added benefit, the female invests but little into the embryos unless the nutritional condition of the female is sufficient so that the expenditure of fat reserves is likely to produce result. A midwinter time of birth is clearly preferable to a fall delivery, although it is still a far cry from ideal. But a later date is impossible due to the restrictions imposed by hibernation. A fasting mammal supports its metabolic processes primarily by burning stored fat. As hibernation is, in principle, a prolonged fasting period, bears depend on their fat layer as energy fuel during winter sleep. They can not replenish spent bodily resources. As a pregnancy places exceedingly high demands on the mother, the females are forced to cut the gestation short and give birth to tiny, premature young. Still, by the time she leaves the den with her new litter, she will have lost up to 50 perecnt of her fall body weight. If the cubs were at birth just marginally larger than what they are, the mother would be unable to satisfy the nutritional requirements of the fetuses. The

stored fat would not suffice to provide enough energy. The increased demand for protein could only be met by breakdown of their mother's muscle tissue. Ultimately, this would put her life at risk.

Newborn brown bear cubs are almost naked, are blind, are eight to nine inches long and weigh about a pound. Of all the higher mammals, bears give birth to the smallest young in relation to the size of the mother. In the darkness of the den, the tiny cubs move without the sow's assistance toward her almost hairless belly, which, when the mother is curled into a fetal position, becomes part of a natural, warm pouch. A female brown bear has six nipples, four on

the chest, two on her lower abdomen. The newborn offspring locate the nipples of their mother by migrating towards heat. The breast milk of bears is very rich. In polar bears, it contains up to forty-eight percent fat. In Black Bears and Grizzlies, average fat content in the milk is twenty-two to twenty-four percent. In the ensuing months, the cubs gain about a pound per fortnight. In mid-May, when they emerge with their mother

from their winter home, the young weigh ten to fifteen pounds. By the end of their first summer, they have multiplied their weight again. Along the Brooks River, the record is held by a juvenile bear, which brought to scale 125 pounds at the tender age of nine months.

As a rule, the cubs remain with their mother for two and a half years. At the start of their third summer, the sow, often quite suddenly, quits tolerating her cubs around her and drives them away. As the female is frequently observed soon after in the company of a male, it is assumed that the aggressive behavior on the part of the mother toward her own offspring is the result of hormonal change.

About fifteen percent of females keep their progeny for a third year. Occasionally, some fortunate cubs remain four years under the protective maternal wing.

The sow nurses her cubs for at least two years, although the young already supplement their diet with grasses, roots, herbs, and fish in their first summer. Nursing bouts

usually last from six to eight minutes when the cubs are still small. Later, as they grow older, stronger, and more efficient at suckling, nursing bouts are shorter, lasting from three to four minutes.

Sexual Maturity and Life Expectancy

Male brown bears reach sexual maturity at the age of seven years. In general, though, the animal is unable to pass on its genetic material to the next generation until several breeding periods later. Its body size far from the adult maximum, such a young boar stands no chance in a confrontation with a fully-grown rival. Females mature sexually one or two years earlier, and some sows experience motherhood at the young age of five years. However, these first attempts at raising offspring are rarely blessed with success.

An adult brown bear lives in a world with no natural enemies but his own kind. The mortality rate among fully-grown animals is low, about five percent a year. By contrast, the chance of survival for bears in their first years of life look rather grim. Almost one-third of the cubs do not live to see a second summer. Between ten and twenty percent of the yearlings disappear. Some twenty-five to thirty percent of the subadults released into independence by their mother never attain sexual maturity. Most deaths

are caused either by another bear or by malnutrition. The most critical phase for a young bruin is spring. After the long period of hibernation, the fat deposits of the cubs are depleted and those of the mother are at their annual minimum. In the long weeks following the harsh winter, even low-quality food is in short supply, and large boars claim what little is available.

In the wild, bears may live to the age of thirty years. And the occasional, resilient individual, as proven by the Brooks River Methuselah "Diver", even walks a few tentative steps into its fourth decade of life. In general, though, a bear that has seen more than twenty summers is regarded as old. The life expectancy of captive animals is substantially higher, due to excellent medical care and a well-balanced diet. A female brown bear kept in a zoo holds the record for the oldest known bruin that ever lived. She died at forty-seven years old.

Home Ranges and Hierarchy

Brown bears do occupy home ranges, but they do not defend them against their own kind. Thus, by definition, these home ranges are not territories and should not be confused with such. Maintaining territorial boundaries makes sense only if the advantage obtained by exclusive exploitation of the resources contained in the

area justifies the energy expended and the risk involved in defending these boundaries. Because brown bears travel across vast tracts of land to satisfy their nutritional needs, and because different areas in their environment provide food at varying times of the year, the defense of such a large expanse of country would be impossible. However, if the resource is both limited and concentrated in a small area, such as a kill, carrion, or even a small but rich berry patch, bears will fight competitors fiercely.

The annual home ranges of bears vary greatly in form and size, depending on topography and the food sources contained within the area. As adult males range widely during the mating season in search of sows in estrus, their home ranges are substantially larger than those of females. On the Kodiak Archipelago, the island group separated from the Alaska Peninsula by twenty-seven miles of rough ocean, the home ranges encompass fifty to eighty-five square miles for fully-grown boars, and eleven to thirty-five square miles for adult females.

As bears are solitary animals by nature, their social system is relatively simple in structure. Sows with cubs form family units that exist for two to three years. All other ties between individual bears are relatively loose and prevail for a short time only. During the breeding season, the sexual partners spend a few weeks in close togetherness at the very most. After a female bear severs the family knot by displaying intolerance toward her offspring, the siblings frequently feed, sleep and travel together during their first summer and fall on their own. Often they also den together and finally separate in the next spring. In some cases, the ties between the siblings persist for yet another full year. However, there is no firm, stable nexus connecting these subadults. The juveniles separate from time to time, usually joining up again within a few hours, but occasionally they do not reunite for several days.

Size and aggressiveness determine the position of a bear in the hierarchy. The huge adult males claim the very top of the rank. On the ladder of hierarchy they are followed by maternal females, which owe their elevated position in bear society to their tendency to behave aggressively whenever they perceive their cubs in danger. The very bottom rank is held by three- and four-year-old, independent subadults. Conflicts over mating privileges or food resources occur mostly between animals of similar size. Even then, the majority of confrontations are restricted to threat displays occasionally backed up by a few powerful blows from strong paws. Serious injuries are the exception. The hierarchy is not always apparent even when bears congregate in great numbers in a small area. Dominant bears display less tolerance toward subordinate animals when the food supply is meager. At the peak of the salmon run, when the waters

abound with fish, bears of different size are occasionally observed peacefully catching salmon next to each other.

The Biology of Bears

Bears are unusual members of the order *Carnivora*, the meat eaters. Only polar bears do justice to the standard conception of a carnivore by predominantly leading the life of a predator, hunting seals and other marine mammals. For all other bear species, meat or fish is of comparatively minor significance. The diet of most brown bears is to more than eighty percent vegetable. Coastal brown bear are an exception in this regard. Because they stuff themselves with salmon during the summer and fall, plants play a much smaller role in their feeding habits. But in the spring, even the bears on the Alaska Peninsula are forced to rely primarily on flowers, grasses, sedges, and roots for sustenance, as little other food is available. In the fall, in most parts of the peninsula, the bears supplement their diet extensively with blue-, soap-, salmon-, and cranberries. Some bears, in fact, seem to prefer berries to fish late in the season.

The diet of bears defies generalization, as the animals are highly opportunistic in their feeding habits. They utilize every resource available. Bears eat carrion, and take the prey of other carnivores. And

despite their huge bulk and ungainly appearance, they are successful hunters. In some areas in Interior Alaska, as much as forty percent of all moose and caribou calves fall victim to brown bears.

Due to their mass and their diet, bears differ greatly from typical carnivores such as cats and dogs. For instance, bears walk on the soles of their hind feet, a posture called "plantigrade", whereas cats and dogs have "digitigrade" feet in which only the toes touch the ground. Digitigrade feet enable the animal to run faster by lengthening the stride. Bears, by contrast, are rather mediocre sprinters despite the fact that they are able to move at speeds of up to thirty-five miles per hour. For a long-distance chase, they are much too heavy. Nobody would call them fleet-footed; their legs are relatively short, yet have a much wider range of motion than the limbs of typical runners. As they are packed heavily with muscle, the stout forelegs of bears are capable of producing great force. The mobility and strength of their limbs are of great importance for bears in their search for food, such as digging for roots. The animals may not be able to escape danger by fleeing, but as a rule they are quite capable of defending themselves through brute force.

The largely vegetarian diet of a bear seems to contradict our preconceived image of a predator. On the basis of their food preferences, their ancestors would have matched our idea of carni-

vores much better. Most of the living members of the family *Ursidae*, the Bears, can be traced back to a small fox-like creature that lived about five to ten million years ago. In the course of evolution, morphological characteristics developed that enabled the

animals to concentrate increasingly on plants in their diet. In contrast to specialized carnivores, bears have a greater number of molar teeth, which are also enlarged and cusped to crush grasses and roots. It is more difficult to extract energy from plant matter than flesh, so the intestines of bears in relation to body length are much longer than those of wolves or lions. However, their digestive tract is still short if compared with ruminants such as cows or sheep. As they lack the support of the necessary symbiotic microorganisms, they are also unable to break down the cellulose in plant cell walls.

Predators always live between the extremes: periods of gluttony alternate with times of hunger. After a meal, days may pass before a new kill is made. Thus, many predators supplement their diet to some degree with vegetables, and especially fruit. Bears have made this former dietary addition their main course. The success of the omnivorous nourishment shows in the fact that the present-day members of the family *Ursidae* are substantially larger than their ancestors. Under optimal conditions such as those found on the Alaska Peninsula or on the Kodiak Archipelago, brown bears may weigh more than fifteen hundred pounds. Along with the polar bear, these gargantuan animals are the largest terrestrial carnivores in the world.

Hibernation

In late fall, before the bitter cold of winter descends upon the land, brown bears enter dens and go into hibernate. In the northern part of their distribution area, the animals may spend sixty percent of their lives in deep sleep. By contrast, in mild winters in southern Alaska, such as on the Kodiak Archipelago, some males do not retreat at all to protected quarters to renounce the outside worlds for a few months. However, these individuals show no exuberance either. Instead, they are relatively sedentary, and appear extremely lethargic at times. During the worst weeks, they spend most of their time sleeping, bedded under trees or in the shelter of bushes.

Shortage of food is the driving force behind the retreat from active life. As the end of the year draws closer,

the land provides less and less in terms of high-energy victuals. Eventually, bears are unable to even come close to replacing the calories burned in the search for nourishment. Hence, there is an advantage to conserving energy by reducing all bodily functions to a minimum, and letting metabolism burn on low flame. Depending on gender, family status, and age, bears enter their dens at different times. Pregnant females and sows with cups belong to the vanguard. They are followed by subadults, then by adult females without progeny. The last to resign themselves to the long sleep ahead are the dominant boars. In spring, the animals emerge in reverse order. Strong competition for the meager resources available in the months bordering winter is the reason for the variance in time spent in hibernation.

Along the Brooks River, the last bears leave for their winter home in November. The animals move into the surrounding mountains to excavate a den somewhere at higher elevation where temperatures remain below freezing all through the win-

ter. As a rule, the den is quite small, consisting of a short tunnel one to two yards long and a chamber barely large enough for the bear to turn around inside. Many excavation dens collapse in spring when the soil thaws. Even those that survive the summer undamaged are rarely reused in the next winter. Although bears are faithful to the area in which they dig their dens, they usually excavate a new hole every fall.

During winter sleep, the body temperature of a brown bear drops only six to sixteen degrees Fahrenheit. The pulse slows from fifty beats per minute to about ten. The rate of metabolism is cut by a half. Still, while lost in deep slumber, a bear loses as much as thirty percent of its body weight, a lactating female as much as forty percent. In comparison with small hibernators such as marmots or ground squirrels, such numbers are astronomically high. The bodily reserves burned by these rodents during the cold part of the year are reasonably small, as their body temperature chills to within a few degrees of freezing or may even dip below the freezing point, and their heart reaches only one to two percent of its summertime performance. However, the higher metabolic rate during a bear's winter sleep is essential; otherwise pregnancy could not take place during hibernation.

To balance the weight lost over the winter, bears must consume large quantities of high-energy foods in summer

and fall to accumulate ample fat deposits. A healthy bear late in the season is extremely obese. The total bodyweight of a pregnant female at denning time is made up of as much as sixty percent fat.

Bears do not drink or eat during hibernation. Neither do they defecate or urinate. They recycle metabolic waste products almost completely, rebuilding proteins so that the muscle mass remains constant or shows only a gradual decline, whereas most other mammals show a continuous loss of body protein when fasting. Unlike humans, the bones of bears remain strong even in the absence of physical strain. The recycling of waste products also prevents the accumulation of metabolic waste from reaching toxic concentrations. These physiological characteristics have made bears a popular subject in medical research, as it is hoped that the results will provide new treatments and medication for diseases such as osteoporosis and kidney failure.

Taxonomy of Bears

The brown bear, *Ursus arctos*, is the most widespread member of the family *Ursidae*. Its distribution area extends from remote mountain vales in the Pyrenees of Spain across the expanse of Russia to the secluded valleys of the Wind River Range in Wyoming in the United States. According to estimates, total brown bear population worldwide amounts to between 125,000 and 150,000 animals, 50,000 of which live in North America. In total, four subspecies are recognized. Almost all brown bears residing in Canada and the United States, including Alaska, are assigned to the subspecies *Ursus arctos horribilis*. This includes both the grizzly and also the so-called coastal brown bear. In general, brown bears in the interior and the Far North of North America are considered grizzlies. Coastal brown bears inhabit the Alaska Peninsula and also the Pacific Coast from Alaska to British Columbia. Due to a comparatively mild climate, and in particular because of the availability of a high-energy food source during the salmon migration, coastal brown bears surpass grizzlies in body size, attaining leviathan dimensions. However, a division into separate subspecies is not justified biologically, nor does it appear sensible. Any differentiation on a taxonomic level would be arbitrary. The transition is fluid. The assignment of animals to separate subspecies according to the home range would result in individuals living near the invisible frontier being considered coastal brown bears on some days and grizzlies on others, depending on their whereabouts. Due to differences in their genetic code, only those brown bears that inhabit the islands of the Kodiak Archipelago are considered a separate subspecies, *Ursus arctos middendorffi*. Isolated from their mainland

cousins, some characteristics have developed in the course of countless generations by means of which their genotype is today sufficiently distinct to permit to regard these animals as a separate geographic race. However, these differences are minimal. On average, skulls of Kodiak bears are somewhat wider and more massive than those of coastal brown bears. But just as there are Kodiak bears with a relatively narrow head, there are bears on the mainland with a rather round face. The strong similarity in appearance and feeding habits resulted in some confusion even among biologists, as demonstrated by the fact that a few scientific publications still list coastal brown bears and Kodiak bears as members of the same subspecies whereas grizzlies are given its own.

Communication of Bears and Advice about Correct Behavior in Bear Country

As bears are solitary animals, living neither in herds nor packs, social contact between individual animals is relatively small. As there is no need for a communication beyond the very basic, the animals lack a complex body language, and the ability to vocalize is limited to a narrow range of sounds. In absence of need, the morphological features necessary for either never evolved. Thus, the requisite muscles for facial expressions are poorly developed. The

ears are small and unsuited to imparting visual signals. The tail is but a short stump and none the better at conveying a message. Consequently, due to these physical limitations, the communication of bears is more straightforward than in many other animals. It lacks nuances, and intervening steps are frequently skipped. As the animals react to threat without much shilly-shallying, they are considered highly unpredictable by many. However, they are by no means more unpredictable than many other animals. Bears do give signals, but often they are misinterpreted or not recognized as such. Frequently, nervous bears yawn, which is erroneously regarded as the reaction of a bored individual. A bear experiencing extreme stress may be foaming at the mouth, an indication that the animal is walking the thin line separating flight and fight. Such signals indicate that the so-called magic circle of a bear, a personal space of individual diameter, has been violated. Any transgression of a bear's private sphere results either in the withdrawal of the animal or in the forceful removal of the intruder.

Although the communication skills are somewhat restricted, bears are extremely adaptable animals and curious by nature. They inspect their environment at all times, a behavior that plays an important part in the search for food. In experiments in zoos, bears investigated curios such as toys in their enclosures more intensely and for a longer time

than primates did. Every individual bear has a character of its own. Distinct animals react differently to environmental stimuli. Depending on its state of mind at the time, the same bear may display diametrically opposite behavior in similar situations.

Due to their individuality, it is difficult to give advice on how to react upon encountering a bear. As the animals are endowed by nature with physical strength, speed, and agility far superior to man, the goal of our behavior in bear country should be to avoid confrontation. This can be achieved most effectively if food is treated with utmost care and is stored properly so that no bear can get to it. It should never, under any circumstances, be stashed in or near the tent. Because surprised or frightened animals sometimes act according to the motto that attack is the best mode of defense, one is strongly advised to walk through the wildlands with eyes wide open, with ears pricked, talking or singing loudly at places with low visibility to announce one's presence. As a rule, bears show little interest in people and do not consider us two-legged beings as potential prey. If they are given the chance to avoid man, in most instances they will take it.

However, we should never forget that we are but guests in the realm of the bear, and as such we should show respect for the animal. Ideally, the impact of our presence on the behavior of the bears should not be felt. The animals should be allowed to pursue their activities undisturbed at all times. The best photographic opportunities arise when the bears are relaxed, totally ignoring us. If we act obtrusively, the animals only become nervous and wander off.

In bear country, one's safety can never be taken for granted and is by no means guaranteed. However, the risk of being mauled by a bear is much smaller than the hazards of traffic we take upon ourselves almost every day.

The Life History of Salmon

Five species of salmon spawn in the clear, oxygen-rich brooks and streams along the Pacific Coast of Canada and Alaska. In July, large schools of sockeye salmon (*Oncorhynchus nerka*) arrive in the Brooks River. In September, late-arriving sockeye mingle with a small run of coho salmon (*Oncorhynchus kisutch*). Adult sockeye and coho salmon newly arrived in the rivers are bright silver. In the course of time spend in freshwater, these breeding animals change in color. Both sexes turn pale to olive-green on the head and maroon to red on the back and sides. Sockeye salmon grow to thirty-three inches in length and four to eight pounds in weight. The coho is bigger, reaching a maximal length of forty inches and a weight of twelve pounds.

Salmon are anadromous, meaning they spend a large part of their lives in the open sea and enter freshwater systems to spawn. After hatching, juvenile sockeye salmon spend between one and three years in freshwater before migrating down to the ocean as silvery smolt weighing only a few ounces. The fish stay in the sea for two to four years. Then, as mature salmon, they travel thousands of miles from their feeding areas to spawn in the very stream where they were born, completing the cycle of life. Upon entering freshwater, salmon do not feed anymore and depend on their stores of fat for sustenance. Their energy demands are so great that even their scales are absorbed. After spawning, their bodily reserves are totally depleted; shortly thereafter all die.

The chances are slim that a newly hatched salmon will ever reproduce. Depending on her size, a female sockeye salmon produces from 2,000 to 4,500 eggs. Only about ten of the young fry born reach sexual maturity; not more than two or three succeed in returnings to their natal stream to spawn.

References

Books

Alaska Geographic Society: Alaska's Bears, Alaska Geographic Volume 20, No. 4, Anchorage, AK 1993
Herrero, Steven: Bear Attacks: Their Causes and Avoidance, Lyons & Burford, Publishers, New York, NY 1985
Lynch, Wayne: Bears—Monarchs of the Northern Wilderness, The Mountaineers, Seattle, WA 1993
Murie, Adolph: The Grizzlies of Mt. McKinley, University of Washington Press, Seattle, WA 1987
Rockwell, David: Giving voice to bear, Roberts Rinehart Publishers, Niwot, CO 1991
Smith, David: Backcountry Bear Basics, The Mountaineers, Seattle, WA 1997
Stirling, Ian (Con. Ed.): Bears—Majestic Creatures of the wild), Rodale Press, Emmaus, PA 1993
Walker, Tom; Aumiller, Larry: River of Bears, Voyageur Press, Stillwater, MN 1993

Papers

Barnes, Victor G: The influence of salmon availability on movements and range of brown bears on southwest Kodiak Island. Int. Conf. Bear Res. and Manage. 8:305-313, 1990

Barnes, Victor G., Jr.; Smith, Roger B.: Survival and productivity of female brown bears on Kodiak Island, Alaska. Progress Report, Kodiak Brown Bear Research and Habitat Maintenance Trust 1992
Barnes, Victor G., Jr.; Smith, Roger B.: Cub Adoption by brown bears, Ursus arctos middendorffi on Kodiak Island, Alaska. Canadian Field-Naturalist 107(3):365-367, 1993
Barnes, Victor G: Brown bear-human interactions associated with deer hunting on Kodiak Island. Int. Conf. Bear Res. and Manage. 9(1):63-73, 1994
Miller, Sterling D.: Impact of increased bear hunting on survivorship of young bears. Wildl. Soc. Bull. 18:462-467, 1990
Miller, Sterling D.: Population Management of Bears in North America. Int. Conf. Bear Res. and Manage. 8:357-373, 1990
Miller, Sterling D.; Ballard, Warren B.: Analysis of an effort to increase moose calf survivorship by increased hunting of Brown bears in south-central Alaska. Wildl. Soc. Bull. 20:445-454, 1992
Sellers, Richard A.: Dynamics of a hunted brown bear population at Black Lake, Alaska. Annual Progress Report, Alaska Department of Fish and Game, Division of Wildlife Conservation 1993
Sellers, Richard A.; Miller, Sterling D.; Smith, Tom S.; Potts, Rick: Population dynamics and habitat partitioning of a naturally regulated brown bear population on the coast of Katmai National Park. Annual Progress Report, Alaska Department of Fish and Game, Division of Wildlife Conservation 1993
Sellers, Richard A.; Aumiller, Larry D.: Brown Bear population characteristics at McNeil River, Alaska. Int. Conf. Bear Res. and Manage. 9(1):283-293, 1994
Smith Roger B.; Barnes, Victor G.; Van Daele, Lawrence J.: Brown bear-human conflicts in the Kodiak Archipelago, Alaska. Bear-People Conflicts - Proc. of a Symposium on Management Strategies, Northwest Territories Dept. of Renew. Res. 1989
Swenson, Jon: Sweden and Norway: Historic and present status of the brown bear in Scandinavia. International Bear News Vol.3, No. 3, 1994
Van Daele, Lawrence J.; Barnes, Victor G.; Smith Roger B.: Denning characteristics of Brown Bears on Kodiak Island, Alaska. Int. Conf. Bear Res. and Manage. 8:257-267, 1990

Acknowledgements

Over the last fifteen years, I have spent several months every year on the Alaska Peninsula and along the Brooks River to take the images reproduced in this book, and to gain the experiences that later found entry into the manuscript. While working on the project, I was blessed with the good fortune of winning close friends in the area. Without their support in word and deed, numerous trips would have been impossible. I am especially indebted to Calvin and Pam Riddle in Naknek. Their door always

stood open to me, and they went through a lot of trouble to provide assistance when I was in need of help. Without the support of Anita Maas, a bad cold would have foiled all my plans for the fall of 1996. Lynn Shawback from King Salmon proved a competent and reliable pilot even under difficult conditions.

For some undertakings, I depended on the assistance of my fellow photographers. Russ Gutshall and Theo Allofs willingly lent me a hand in setting up the underwater equipment. It is thanks to the help of

Michelle Waye that the images of the newborn bear cubs came to be.

Some knowledge can be gained from reading books and scientific papers. However, a thorough understanding of bears requires a hands-on approach; one must spend time out in the wildlands with the animals. To interpret the impressions gained while being in the realm of the bears, I benefited greatly from discussions with biologists, who have worked with bears professionally for many years. My knowledge about

bears has profited immensely from long talks with Larry Aumiller, Richard Sellers, John Westlund, and Larry Van Daele, who time and again patiently answered my questions and shared their experiences with me.

For untiring proofreading and constructive criticism of the manuscript in its various stages, I am much indebted to my father Reinhard Breiter.

Since the first edition of this book, the list of people I am indebted too has grown: without the assistance of John

Rogers and Chuck Keim my extended sojourns on the Katmai Coast would have been impossible. Tony Lara provided invaluable assistance and friendship in and around Kodiak. Dean Andrew, Willy Fulton, and Rolan Ruoss got me out to the bears many times through all kinds of weather. Robert Ponté kept my mobile home running reliably. Missy Epping and Jim Gavin got me home from a photo shoot in Brooks Camp in time for my daughter's birth.

Above all I am indebted to my wife Laurel Snyder, who is a limitless source of encouragement and patience, even when I again depart for a prolonged trip to the bears. And last but not least I am thankful to my daughters Aislyn and Kiri Anne. Aislyn called me home from Katmai by means of her early arrival before the weather turned too nasty. Both supported me with their smiles and cheerful disposition during the long hours of redesigning the book.

Matthias Breiter, Kenora, Ontario, March 2008

About the images

All of the images of bears depict animals living in Katmai National Park, Alaska, with the following exceptions: The photographs on the pages 34-36 and 37 top left and 37 top right, showing newborn bear cubs, and pages 85 right and 86 left, depicting the bear with mouth agape, were taken on the Olympic Game Farm in Sequim, WA. The pictures on pages 64-67, portraying a female nursing her cubs, were photographed in the McNeil River State Game Sanctuary on the northern boundary of Katmai National Park.